D1403577

More Civil War
Curiosities

Also by Webb Garrison

Atlanta and the War
Civil War Curiosities
Civil War Trivia and Fact Book
Great Stories of the American Revolution
A Treasury of Civil War Tales
A Treasury of White House Tales

More Civil War Curiosities

Webb Garrison

RUTLEDGE HILL PRESS ®
Nashville, Tennessee

Published in Nashville, Tennessee, by Rutledge Hill Press, Inc., 211 Seventh Avenue North, Nashville, Tennessee 37219. Distributed in Canada by H. B. Fenn & Company, Ltd., 34 Nixon Road, Bolton, Ontario L7E 1W2. Distributed in the United Kingdom by Verulam Publishing, Ltd., 152a Park Street Lane, Park Street, St. Albans, Hertfordshire AL2 2AU.

Typography by E. T. Lowe, Nashville, Tennessee

ISBN   1-56865-876-1

Contents

Part Three: Notorious and Nonesuch

Part Four: The Money Trail

Introduction

During a delightful swing through Virginia and Pennsylvania, my wife and I stopped at every Civil War battlefield we could find. Many of them include gift shops with lots of great books, so it was natural to talk with park rangers who were well informed on the war and specific battlefields. When asked about something off the beaten path, at least half a dozen of them pulled out a fast-moving volume by Burke Davis. Since *Our Incredible Civil War* has been on my bookshelf for longer than I like to remember, I shook my head at offers of this one.

Responding to this reaction, in shop after shop, someone said that a new volume in this genre was greatly needed. I heartily agreed, since Davis put his collection of unusual facts into print in 1960.

As a result of these encounters I prepared the manuscript of *Civil War Curiosities* in 1994. This volume wasn't sixty days old before booksellers with whom I talked began telling me that they'd like to have a follow-up volume. *More Civil War Curiosities* is the result of this deep interest in unusual aspects of our nation's bloodiest and most colorful struggle.

If the June 1865 surrender of Kirby-Smith's forces is taken as the last hurrah of the Confederacy, then the war lasted almost fifty months. During that time an average of more than 250 military events occurred daily. Millions of men and thousands of encounters produced a multitude of extraordinary things.

Numerous chapters here focus upon events or emphases that have been neglected—maybe because they're hard to locate. Except in these pages, it is all but impossible to find more than an occasional reference to banishment or deportation. If friendly fire during the Civil War has been treated earlier anywhere, I've failed to find it. Because a fellow put his life on the line when he so much as whispered about "fragging," the chapter dealing with this intramural sport of soldiers is comparatively short.

Does this collection exhaust possibilities for compilations of its sort? No. Plenty of other fast-moving, offbeat topics aren't touched here because there's a limit to the number of pages that can be used. Whether you're a lifelong addict or just beginning to get acquainted with the Civil War, you'll find a trove of conversation-starters here. Maybe you'll want to use what few blank spots there are in this volume to add notes about other unusual aspects of the war that was launched in a fervent bid to preserve the Union.

Part One

The Unusual and Bizarre

In recent decades the phrase "friendly fire" has been elevated into nearly universal use. To err is human, and the fighting men of the Civil War on both sides were as human as they come. So logically a struggle lasting more than fourteen hundred days would include many instances of friendly fire.

The chapter that follows which deals tersely with friendly fire has come from a wide reading over a period of years. To find out more about this aspect of the conflict, the only way is to stumble across it through general reading. There are no sources other than the compilation included here. Much the same thing can be said about banishment, deportation, and fragging. Be prepared, therefore, for a few surprises in the pages to come.

Self-taught detective Allan Pinkerton (seated, right) "smelled trouble" when he met Rose Greenhow O'Neal for the first time. [LIBRARY OF CONGRESS]

1

Banishment and Deportation

During colonial days, a persistent troublemaker was likely to be banished from the colony. Widely practiced, the punishment was borrowed from the Old World, where lawmakers didn't hesitate to engage in the wholesale deportation of convicts. Maybe because this punishment was linked with British tyranny, the Founding Fathers steered shy of it. The Constitution refers to numerous types of punishments, but banishment and deportation are not among them. Constitutional silence, however, did not inhibit Federal and Confederate leaders, both political and military, as the record shows.

Pioneer detective Allan Pinkerton was sometimes called "a man who was born chock full of suspicions about his own parents." Whether or not that assessment is correct, he had been in and around Washington only a short time before he was sure that someone in the capital was providing a steady flow of vital information to the enemy. Surveillance plus checks of letters and telegrams soon implicated Mrs. Rose Greenhow O'Neal, an attractive widow whose conversation and other charms were fabled.

On August 23, 1861, Pinkerton placed her under house arrest. When he felt that he had confirmation of his suspicions, he managed to have her taken to the Old Capitol Prison. This Sixteenth Street building was once the seat of the Federal government but had been converted recently into a house of detention. Rose Greenhow O'Neal was escorted there by a military guard.

It was not difficult to discover how O'Neal had managed to gain access to reports and recommendations that came from the highest levels of government. Her parties were the talk of Washington, attended by everyone who was anyone. No one knew how many highly placed officials she had entertained, but the list was believed to be long and very, very heavy with brass.

A large packet of love letters was discovered during a search of her home. Uniformly signed only with the initial "H," they may have been penned by Sen. Henry Wilson of Massachusetts. The evidence was not conclusive, since the cunning widow may have forged the missives in an attempt to involve Wilson should she be challenged about her activities.

Established in the Old Capitol Prison with her eight-year-old daughter and a few other women, the widow O'Neal was a political prisoner in the custody of the Department of State. Even so, she boldly continued her correspondence with Confederates. Much evidence supports the view that the Federal debacle at Bull Run stemmed in part from the fact that O'Neal had informed Brig. Gen. P. G. T. Beauregard of the Federals' plans.

That she was guilty of aiding and abetting the enemy, there was not a shadow of doubt. Yet no one, from Lincoln to the midlevel clerks in the State Department, wanted to initiate action against her. If O'Neal were to be tried in court, all sorts of embarrassing secrets were likely to emerge. Whether or not they had shared her bed at times, men who had confided secrets to her were likely to have extremely red faces if she should take the witness stand.

After a shakeup in the Lincoln administration, the responsibility for political prisoners was shifted to the War Department. Brig. Gen. John A. Dix and Judge Edwards Pierrepont were chosen as commissioners to examine civilians held in custody. Soon they were aided by the Bureau of Military Justice, headed by Judge Advocate General Joseph Holt.

Dix, Pierrepont, and Holt—along with Secretary of War Edwin M. Stanton—held only one conference on Rose O'Neal. She was guilty of treason. If tried, she would be convicted and sentenced to hang. Before the noose could be placed around her lovely neck, however, she was sure to talk . . . and talk . . . and talk. Her revelations would prove even more embarrassing than the July 1861 defeat at Manassas Gap, Virginia. In this dilemma, a secret top-level decision was made. Instead of giving O'Neal her day in court, she would be banished from the Union for the duration of the conflict.

By the time the judge advocate general had trumped up a vague legal precedent for the unconstitutional punishment, two friends and allies of the prisoner joined O'Neal in the Sixteenth Street

Joseph Holt considered O'Neal to be guilty but didn't know what to do with her. [NICOLAY AND HAY, ABRAHAM LINCOLN]

prison. Mrs. C. V. Baxley and Mrs. Rosanna Augusta Heath Morris were neither as beautiful nor as clever as O'Neal, but they too were dangerous to the safety of the republic. Hence they shared the fate of their friend and colleague.

In June 1862 an officer of the First U.S. Volunteer Cavalry, heading a guard of six men, reached the Old Capitol. Accompanied by the warden, they led the three women to Fort Monroe, Virginia. After a period of detention in the only Virginia installation to remain in Federal hands throughout the war, the trio solemnly swore not to return to Union soil. They were then led to the Confederate lines and ceremonially released.

As the central figure in the first U.S. case in which a citizen was banished, O'Neal occupies a special niche in the annals of the period. She subsequently went to England and returned on the blockade-runner *Condor*. Nearing the coast, the ship was forced aground by vessels of the Federal blockade. Jumping from her ship to avoid capture, O'Neal drowned near Wilmington, North Carolina, on October 1, 1864.

Deportation consisted of involuntary physical departure from home, but it did not require deportees to leave the country. Where

As its name implies, Old Capitol Prison was once the Capitol of the United States. [NATIONAL ARCHIVES]

martial law was declared, it may have been legal. Few commanders, however, bothered to make formal declarations of martial law; they simply exercised absolute command over areas they controlled.

No other woman attracted as much notice as did Rose Greenhow O'Neal, but numbers of them were banished or deported by leaders on both sides. One of the first to be forced from her home was Phoebe Drew of Fairview, Arkansas. Her husband, a Unionist, fled into the swamps. Hence Phoebe and her three small children were made to leave the state in June 1861.

In 1862, as military commander of New Orleans, Union Maj. Gen. Benjamin F. Butler became incensed when Mrs. Eugenia Philips was seen to laugh at the moment a Union officer's funeral train was passing her home. Butler immediately sent her into exile on Ship Island off the Mississippi Gulf Coast as punishment for "unpatriotic levity."

Near Memphis, Belle Edmonton was banished in 1863 from the region by Union officials. Her crime consisted of having waved a Confederate flag at a boatload of prisoners.

In divided Missouri, Puss Whitty of Jackson County was reputed to have shot a Federal lieutenant in the arm before fleeing into the woods. When authorities captured her, she was banished from the state.

At Vicksburg on December 27, 1863, Brig. Gen. James B. McPherson banished five women. Having "acted disrespectfully toward the President," Kate Barnett, Ella Barrett, Laura Latham, Ellen Martin, and a Mrs. Moore were ordered to leave Union lines within forty-eight hours.

McPherson followed with a warning that "all persons, male or female, who by word or deed or by implication do insult or show disrespect to the President, the Government, or the flag of the United States, or to any officer or soldier of the United States shall be fined, banished, or imprisoned, according to the grossness of the offense."

Drastic punishment of men by Federal officers started at least as early as August 1861. Brig. Gen. John Pope, who then controlled part of Missouri, decided that he'd seen too much of irregulars and bushwhackers. A proclamation reprinted in the *Washington Republican* banned illegal assemblages and warned that all persons "taken in arms against the United States" would be sent to Mexico.

At Saint Louis, Maj. Gen. Henry W. Halleck, who had declared martial law, banished merchant Samuel Engler from the Department of Missouri in January 1862. One month later editor Edmund J. Ellis of the *Boone County Standard* was banished from the state.

Commanding the Army of Virginia in July 1862, Pope seems to have consulted Abraham Lincoln. Apparently with the president's approval he issued General Order No. 11. Terms of the proclamation required Virginia citizens to take an oath of loyalty to the United States. Failure to take such an oath, said the military commander, would bring immediate punishment: "Those who refuse shall be conducted south beyond the extreme pickets of this army and be notified if found again anywhere within our lines or at any point in the rear they will be considered spies and subject to extreme rigor of military law."

On April 13, 1863, Maj. Gen. Ambrose Burnside was commander of the Department of the Ohio. From his headquarters he ordered Southern sympathizers deported to Confederate lines. Anyone found guilty of aiding the enemy, added the Union general, would receive an automatic death penalty.

During the first week of 1864 persons identified only as making up "a band of Southern sympathizers" were banished from Knoxville, Tennessee.

In 1861 Virginia lawmakers passed an ordinance directed at "persons holding office under the Government of the United States." All such were labeled as aliens and enemies and ordered to be "forever banished from the state" as traitors. Within days, editors of the *New Orleans Delta* were rejoicing at the "contemplated expulsion of all citizens of the United States from the Confederated States."

There was no systematic way to enforce this plan, so no one knows how many people were ordered to leave Confederate soil. At San Antonio in August 1861, records show that J. R. Ritchliff and W. P. M. Means appeared before a military commission and were required to leave the country.

Undeterred by the difficulty of enforcement, in November 1862 the Confederate Senate began debate on a special bill that would authorize Jefferson Davis to order all persons "who were loyal, and adhered to the United States Government" to depart from Confederate soil within forty days. This treatment of "alien enemies," conceded Confederate Secretary of War G. W. Randolph, "was equivalent to banishment."

Military commanders had enforcement power that civilian lawmakers lacked. Hence most enforced removals occurred in occupied territory. This process began shortly after the fall of Fort Sumter and continued for the duration. Strangely, it has had little attention and cannot be documented by use of standard indexes except when names of commanders and locations are known.

At Key West, where firm Union control never relaxed, on September 16, 1861, Bvt. Maj. William H. French issued a proclamation giving civilians sixty days in which to take an oath of allegiance to the United States. All citizens of the island, their families, and the families of residents who had relatives in Confederate service were told they'd be removed if they did not take the required oath.

In Missouri, site of more battles than any other state except Virginia and Tennessee, Confederates and Confederate sympathizers around Saint Louis were herded into Camp Jackson. In December 1861 they were given the choice of taking an oath of allegiance to the Union or being banished into Southern territory.

Brig. Gen. Thomas Ewing Jr. of Ohio was responsible for the first mass deportation of civilians. Commander of the District of the Border, which included part of Missouri, he issued his General Order No. 11 during the spring of 1863. Under its terms, residents of four Missouri counties believed to include Southern sympathizers were ordered to leave their homes. Hundreds of people, including numerous Unionists, obeyed within the fifteen-day grace period Ewing had stipulated. Supported by Lincoln, the general from Ohio promised to execute all violators of this order.

No one knows exactly how many were involved in this mass deportation. It excited indignation and anger in the North as well as in the South, however. Artist George Caleb Bingham protested Ewing's action with a large painting depicting the flight of the innocents.

In July 1862 the Federal provost marshal of Memphis, Tennessee, ordered "all persons connected with the rebel army or government to leave the city with their families within five days." At least 130 residents of the river city "were provided with passes to go to the South." Though his name was not directly attached to the directive, Maj. Gen. William Tecumseh Sherman—a foster brother of Thomas Ewing—was responsible for the deportation.

Simultaneously, the Federal commander sent his Forty-sixth Ohio Infantry Regiment to destroy houses, farms, and crops for fifteen miles below the city on the west bank of the Mississippi River. River boats soon came under fire from marksmen concealed on riverbanks. In reprisal, Sherman announced that each such incident would cause families of ten Confederates to be evicted from the city even if they had taken the oath of allegiance.

Sherman reduced the population of Memphis by at least 130 when he began to banish suspected persons. [LIBRARY OF CONGRESS]

At Louisville, forces under Confederate Brig. Gen. Simon B. Buckner threatened the safety of the city. Alarmed Unionists called a mass meeting and demanded that all men between the ages of eighteen and forty-five enroll for service in militia companies. "All who refuse shall be sent to the North," warned the directive issued by civilians.

In Camden County, North Carolina, Unionists informed Lincoln that they could raise two regiments of volunteers. They'd move to do so, they promised the president, once he gave them permission to drive all Rebel families out of the county.

Civilian threats were sometimes meaningless because there were no enforcement mechanisms. In the case of military officers, among whom Maj. Gen. William Tecumseh Sherman exceeded his peers, enforcement of an order was easy.

Approaching Atlanta, he became incensed upon learning that a textile factory at Roswell flew a French flag. In reprisal for what he considered a subterfuge, he ordered more than four hundred

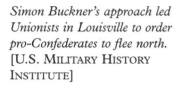

Simon Buckner's approach led Unionists in Louisville to order pro-Confederates to flee north. [U.S. MILITARY HISTORY INSTITUTE]

women employees sent north with their children. The terminus of their enforced journey by rail was Louisville, where they disappeared from the record.

Another textile factory on Sweetwater Creek near Atlanta employed about half as many women as did the Roswell facilities. These women too were dispatched to the North and dumped into a strange city or cities without money or resources. Like the Roswell women, few of them were able to return home after the war; for practical purposes, they simply vanished.

Once Sherman succeeded in cutting the rail lines into Atlanta, the heavily fortified city fell. He soon announced plans to turn it into a Federal military base that he called "a western Gibraltar." To implement these plans, he said, it was necessary for all civilians to depart immediately. Those who wished to go north could do so; others would be escorted south to the rail station of Rough and Ready and turned loose upon the countryside.

Lt. Col. William G. Le Duc was assigned the job of making—for once—an accurate tally of persons driven from their homes by Sherman's order of September 4, 1864. According to Le Duc's

Ambrose Burnside issued orders forbidding anyone to express Southern sympathies. [NATIONAL ARCHIVES]

records, 1,651 civilians—men, women, and children—were forced to leave Atlanta and go south. Unlike the textile workers from Roswell and Sweetwater Creek, the majority of these people eventually were able to return home.

These mass deportations were dramatic and emotional but relatively unheralded by the press. The banishment of a former Congressman from Ohio, however, attracted far more public interest.

Less than a month after Maj. Gen. Ambrose Burnside had used his Order No. 38 to forbid persons within his Department of the Ohio to express sympathy for the Southern cause, on May 4, 1863, a crowd of twenty thousand gathered to hear a speech by Clement L. Vallandigham. The former officeholder said that he "spit upon the Burnside order and trampled it under his feet." Denouncing Lincoln as a dictator, he called for an armistice that would end the fighting.

Late that night soldiers under Burnside's command broke down the door of Vallandigham's residence and carted him off to a military prison. Tried by a commission of eight officers, he was convicted of "publicly expressing sentiments designed to hinder suppression of rebellion."

Lincoln was placed in the difficult position of deciding whether to support the harsh military verdict or to set it aside. Concluding that the planned punishment of Vallandigham would do more harm than good, he directed that the culprit be banished into Confederate territory.

Placed aboard the gunboat *Exchange* at Cincinnati, the former lawmaker eventually reached the headquarters of the Union army at Murfreesboro, Tennessee. Since he still strongly voiced his loyalty to the Union whose policies he challenged, he found himself unwanted by Secessionists. Ordered off Confederate soil, he made a long and circuitous journey to Canada as the only man banished from both the United States and the Confederate States.

Whether individuals or masses were involved, most forcible evictions were illegal; at best, some could be considered extralegal. Yet emotions ran so high in both the North and the South that few persons protested measures that would not have been tolerated earlier. The brief abolition of habeas corpus in Confederate territory and the repeated abolitions of this right by Federal authorities caused both segments of the divided nation to come perilously close to military dictatorships.

2

Self-Inflicted Casualties

Friendly fire, called by any name, is seldom mentioned in the official records. Letters and diaries of soldiers and occasional newspaper accounts reveal that men began shooting their comrades less than a month after Fort Sumter. They didn't stop until after Appomattox.

During the entire conflict, men in blue and gray turned their muskets or artillery upon their own troops more than sixty times. About half of the documented cases are reported here, in roughly chronological order.

Believing no enemy force to be near, the Third New York Infantry approached a dense forest in the region known as Big Bethel, near Hampton, Virginia, early on the morning of June 10, 1861. Following orders of Maj. Gen. Benjamin F. Butler, every man wore a white band on his left arm to identify him as a member of the Federal force.

Marching along a narrow road in route step, troops led by Col. Frederick Townsend believed themselves to be two hours behind another Federal unit. Brig. Gen. Ebenezer W. Peirce and staff of the Massachusetts militia had joined them at midnight to lead a reconnaissance toward Yorktown.

Suddenly "a well sustained fire of small arms and canister" caught these ninety-day volunteers by surprise. Not until the turmoil subsided did Townsend learn the dreadful truth about the unexpected ambush. Men of an advance party, led by a Lieutenant Colonel Washburne of the First Vermont Infantry, had fired on their comrades. Col. John E. Bendix of the Seventh New York Infantry stopped the shooting as soon as he could.

Townsend submitted two reports about the tragedy. According to the first, two men were killed, three were dangerously wounded, and four officers and twelve privates sustained minor injuries. Townsend's second report indicated that the unplanned engagement between the two groups of Union soldiers led to twenty-nine casualties. They were the first known casualties from friendly fire in the Civil War.

At Big Bethel, the use of green troops in early morning fog, dense woods, and lack of distinctiveness in uniforms proved fatal. This combination, or a variant of it, often linked with heavy smoke or dust, occurred repeatedly. In rare instances, a unit carried a false flag or had no flag.

Many times artillerists unwillingly fired at the enemy over the heads of their own infantry and could only hope that they had aimed high enough to miss them. In the emotional intensity of battle, men often fired without having had a good look at their targets.

Frequently the survivors did not learn until later that the deadly lead and iron rained upon them had come from their comrades. Few summaries of such incidents were published at the time they occurred because the men present were often so horrified at what had taken place that they gave only terse reports concerning casualties—or said nothing at all.

About the time the New Yorkers were being felled by their Vermont colleagues, two additional Federal groups were in motion ten miles southeast of Big Bethel. Both groups had been dispatched to seize the strategic area bordering on Hampton Roads.

One body of troops left their Newport News camp well before daybreak; the other departed from Fort Monroe half an hour later. They encountered each other before the sun came up and each unit fired on the other. Officers attributed the costly blunder to "nervousness of green troops in a dangerous situation" and did not report their casualties.

Fairfax Court House, Virginia, was the scene of several early clashes that were usually classified as skirmishes. According to the *New York Evening Post,* a deadly encounter took place on July 5, 1861. Said the newspaper report published far to the north: "This morning the rebel troops stationed at Fairfax Court-House, Va., were advancing upon the Federal lines, when a regiment of their infantry fired by mistake upon a company of their cavalry, killing seven or eight men and wounding several others."

By mid-July some military analysts were sure that a battle of magnitude would occur shortly, and Manassas Junction, Virginia, seemed the likely spot.

On July 18 the Eleventh Virginia Infantry moved toward the rivulet known as Bull Run. Desultory cannon fire from Federal forces frightened men never before involved in battle. Then soldiers wearing motley uniforms set out to cross the stream.

James Franklin Jr. watched as Brig. Gen. James Longstreet's brigade moved forward to meet the enemy, with many men dressed in civilian garb. Almost simultaneously, Confederate Brig. Gen. Jubal A. Early led the Twenty-fourth Virginia Infantry toward the point of conflict.

Franklin wrote that as Early's men came closer to the conflict, confusion took over: "Just as their line approached the edge of the bushes they mistook our men [of the Eleventh Virginia] for the yanks and some of them fired. Gen. Longstreet, being between his brigade and Gen. Early's line, jumped off his horse to keep from being shot. His horse ran off and we thought the General had been killed." Two years later, Longstreet was wounded by Confederate troops during combat in the Wilderness.

Soon after the first battle of Manassas had begun in earnest, members of the Fourth South Carolina Volunteers mistakenly fired upon the unit known as the Louisiana Tigers. Angry Tigers then wheeled and returned the fire until Maj. Chatham R. Wheat restored order to his troops. Leading the Tigers, officially known as the First Louisiana Special Battalion, Wheat ordered his men to turn their attention to a large body of Federals and to charge at the double. Although the assault proved to be costly, for the moment it stopped the exchange of fire between two Confederate units.

Confederate Allen C. Redwood of the Fifty-fifth Virginia Infantry blamed much of the chaos at Bull Run on the lack of standardized uniforms. "So variegated were the costumes on both sides," he wrote, "that both Confederates and Federals frequently fired upon their own men. There are instances recorded where the colonel of a regiment notified his supporters to which side he belonged before daring to advance in front of them."

Analyzing the carnage, historian Francis Trevelyan Miller added, "Since the South had regiments in gray uniforms and many of the men of the North were clad in gray, fatal mistakes occurred and soldiers fired upon their own friends." No one knows how many men were killed or wounded by friendly fire on July 21, 1861.

Soon afterward a reporter for the *Jefferson City (Mo.) Evening News* described a set of blunders he termed "a second Bethel affair." On September 18 the steamers *War Eagle, White Cloud,* and *Desmoines* set out on an expedition designed to show the flag to Southern sympathizers. Fighting men aboard the river craft were from the Eighteenth, Twenty-second, and Twenty-sixth Indiana Regiments. One contingent of Federals set out for Glasgow, the other for Lexington, Missouri.

The commanders of the separate units were not in communication. Late on the evening of their second day, both leaders sent scouting parties toward Glasgow. Said the newspaper report: "The parties met in the woods, a short distance from where the boats were lying, and the scene at Great Bethel was re-enacted. Mistaking each other for enemies they commenced firing, and for some ten or fifteen minutes the firing was incessant. Before they found out their mistake, three troops of the Eighteenth and one of the Twenty-second were killed, and seven or eight were wounded. Among the wounded was Major [Thomas B.] Tanner of the Twenty-second; the wound is a severe one, and he is not expected to live."

Tanner survived, becoming a lieutenant colonel and taking another serious wound at Stones River. Left on the field this time, he was captured by Confederates under the command of Brig. Gen. St. John R. Liddell.

Three months after Bull Run, another incident was more precisely reported than was the first major battle. Said the *Washington National Intelligencer* on September 30: "This morning, about one o'clock, as some of the Federal regiments were advancing in the neighborhood of Munson's Hill, Va., Colonel Owen's Irish regiment mistook a portion of Colonel [Edward D.] Baker's for secessionists, and commenced firing upon them. The fire was returned, and before the mistake was discovered nine men were killed and about twenty-five wounded. Among the killed were three officers."

Lt. Col. Dennis O'Kane of the Sixty-ninth Pennsylvania Infantry noted the affair in a rare official report. According to him, men of the regiment were aroused at 11:15 P.M. and ordered by Brig. Gen.

Richard Anderson led a confused Confederate assault on Fort Pickens. [LIBRARY OF CONGRESS]

William F. "Baldy" Smith to be moving by midnight. Few officers were then aware of the great danger attached to a night movement of any sort.

To make matters worse, both officers and men "were in entire ignorance of the purpose or direction of the movement," O'Kane noted. The sudden appearance of unidentified skirmishers about 1:30 A.M. led to the deadly exchange of fire between the Federal units.

On the night of October 9, 1861, Confederate Brig. Gen. Richard H. "Fighting Dick" Anderson led about one thousand men and a lone newspaper correspondent to Santa Rosa Island, Florida. By staging his assault before daylight, he hoped to break up the Federal batteries protecting Fort Pickens.

As reported in the *Atlanta Intelligencer,* excited soldiers quickly became disordered. "One cause of the confusion," said the newspaper account, "was the strange land we had to climb over and the deep bogs we had to wade."

Union reinforcements from the fort threw attackers into wild confusion. During their chaotic withdrawal, the newspaper corre-

At Belmont, Missouri, Union forces led by U. S. Grant had the support of gunboats. [HARPER'S HISTORY OF THE CIVIL WAR]

spondent didn't know whether the Confederates had won a victory or suffered a defeat. As published, however, his account was clear concerning a central aspect of the disorganized fray: "*We shot down our own friends in numbers.* Indeed, I think as many of our men were shot by friends as by foes. Night skirmishing is a dangerous business, especially in an unknown country, as was the island of Santa Rosa." Col. Harvey Brown of the Fifth U.S. Artillery estimated Confederate losses during the melee at no fewer than 240 killed or wounded.

According to the *Boston Transcript,* a few hours after the Florida debacle another body of Confederates set out to attack Federal forces in and around Paducah, Kentucky. "The rebels had divided their forces," newspaper readers were informed, "and in the excitement fired into each other. They then fled, each party taking the other for the National cavalry."

Gen. Felix Zollicoffer was killed by a single Federal shot. [LESLIE'S ILLUSTRATED]

At Belmont, Missouri, a new and highly dangerous variable became central to fatal friendly fire. On November 7, 1861, the town became the target of a joint operation by infantry units supported by Federal gunboats.

When the attacking forces withdrew to the safety of the Mississippi River, Col. N. B. Buford and the Twenty-seventh Illinois Infantry were left on shore. Buford and his men set out for Charleston and reached Bird's Point without incident.

Suddenly Buford had to modify his plans, for gunners on the river boats were not aware of his movements. "To avoid the effect of the shells from the gunboats that were beginning to fall among his men," a Federal report said, "he took a blind path to the river" where he was able to board a steamer.

As the fall of 1861 yielded to winter, officers on both sides expressed confidence that there would be no more exchanges of fire between comrades. Their optimism was premature. Close to the spot at which two Federal units fired upon one another near the tip of Virginia's southernmost peninsula, Confederate troops made the same blunder five months later. In its issue of November 16, 1861, the *Memphis Appeal* reported: "Two parties of rebel troops met on the peninsula, above Newport News, Va., and mistook each other for enemies. Brisk firing at once commenced, and a number on each side were killed and wounded before the mistake was found out. Among the killed was Major Bailey, of Mobile."

A new year was barely under way before men learned to their dismay that fatal mistakes had not been eliminated. Opposing forces met on January 19, at Mill Springs, Kentucky, also known as Logan's Cross Road. An observer later said that "a moment or two of wild confusion seemed to be an eternity."

Confederate Brig. Gen. Felix K. Zollicoffer took a quick look at the Federal Fourth Kentucky Regiment and thought it to be one of his own units whose men were firing on their friends. His spurs dug into the sides of his horse so he could quickly rectify the error.

When the general came close to the body whose fire he believed should be redirected, he shouted to its leader and pointed to the left with a warning to change directions. "Of course," Col. Speed S. Fry of the Fourth Kentucky is said to have replied. He then lifted his musket to fire a single shot that dropped Zollicoffer from his saddle.

On February 8, 1862, a joint land-sea force of Federals hit Roanoke Island, North Carolina. They scored a decisive victory at the cost of only 260 casualties. Records and diaries fail to indicate how many of these were caused by Confederates and how many were due to friendly fire.

Spanish-born Col. Edward Ferrero of the Fifty-first New York Volunteers, later a brevet major general, said that he "commanded the men to lie down in order to avoid the shower of bullets from our own troops." These bullets, he wrote, came from men of the Ninth New Jersey and Ninth New York Regiments. With a presence of mind rare under such circumstances, Ferrero directed his bugler to sound "Cease fire!" Once the clear notes of the instrument were heard above the sounds of battle, all the troops in the vicinity stopped firing on their comrades.

One week later another joint force set out to capture Confederate-held Fort Donelson on the Cumberland River. This time, Union

Near Fort Donelson, Union gunners came close to hitting the USS Carondelet. [HARPER'S HISTORY OF THE CIVIL WAR]

gunners were responsible for a gross error that came close to sinking one of their own vessels.

Cmdr. Henry Walke of the USS *Carondelet*—destined to figure in many engagements—penned two short reports. According to them, men aboard the USS *Tyler* fired a shell that exploded a short distance astern of the *Carondelet*. Iron penetrated the casemating of the warship, but it escaped disaster.

At Pea Ridge, Arkansas, confusion of the wildest sort reigned on March 7, 1862. Early in the day's fighting, Federal gunners shelled their own troops. Hours later as dusk approached, both Confederate and Union artillery batteries were for a time trained upon men in blue. A battalion of the Twenty-fifth Illinois Regiment, led by Maj. Frederic Nodine, was hardest hit by the barrage from Federal gunners.

Rival bands of Cherokees had been brought into Confederate service. Those led by Stand Watie came willingly, but others had been coerced into the ranks. During heavy fighting, these groups separated and began firing at one another. Unlike most instances in which soldiers shot their comrades by accident, this action was deliberate. When nightfall brought an end to the day's struggle, *New York Herald* reporter Thomas W. Knox filed a grim report. "In camp on that night," he said, "every thing was in confusion."

Accounts of the *Monitor-Virginia* battle focus on the revolutionary nature of the clash between the two ironclads. Survivors were, however, bitter in their denunciation of both the carelessness and the inaccuracy of the Union gunners.

On Saturday afternoon, March 8, 1862, the CSS *Virginia* steamed into Hampton Roads, heavily defended by Federal batteries on shore. Two tiny gunboats, the *Beaufort* and the *Raleigh,* served as escorts for the mighty vessel.

Almost as soon as she was within the waterway, the *Virginia* headed toward the wooden Federal fleet. When the thirty-gun USS *Cumberland* was rammed, she began taking on water rapidly and sank about 3:30. An hour later, having been forced aground, the USS *Congress* surrendered.

Capt. Franklin Buchanan, commander of the Confederate marauder, saw that the *Congress* would soon sink. Her decks were crowded with seamen, he noted. Hence he signaled for men aboard the *Beaufort* and the *Raleigh* to rescue those about to drown. In addition to the Federals, many aboard the Union vessel were prisoners of war who had survived the heavy shelling of the ironclad.

An estimated twenty to thirty prisoners of war soon crowded into the Confederate gunboats with some of their captors. Union shore batteries then opened up on those who were fleeing from the doomed *Congress.* Almost simultaneously, the guns of the sinking warship were turned on the lifeboats holding both Union and Confederate fighting men.

Lt. Robert D. Minor of the *Virginia* was wounded by what the Confederates denounced as "that foul act of treachery." Displaying little concern for himself, Minor angrily testified that shells from the Federal guns on shore "killed some of their own men, among them a lieutenant."

More friendly fire occurred when the USS *Monitor* arrived the next day. W. F. Keeler, paymaster of the Federal "cheese box on a raft," insisted that two of the twenty-three shots that hit the vessel came from the USS *Minnesota.* Naval gunners seeking to sink the

Confederate vessel aimed too low and blasted the ironclad that had come to rescue them, Keeler said.

Big Bethel, Bull Run, and Pea Ridge provided spectacular demonstrations of friendly fire in engagements on land; hence many commanders learned to take precautions. During three days of fierce fighting at Shiloh, they learned that the problem had not been solved completely.

On April 6, 1862, Federals of the Orleans Guard went into battle wearing splendid dress blue uniforms. When the action became heavy, these men were easy targets for a hail of Confederate bullets. One by one, they turned their uniforms inside out. Yet after this change had been effected, men no longer easily identified as belonging to Union units became targets of comrades still boldly displaying their blue.

Viewed from the perspective of Richmond, casualties among the Orleans Guard were minor in importance compared with the loss of one man in gray. Widely known as the South's most able commander, Gen. Albert Sidney Johnston was struck by a nearly spent minié ball while directing front-line operations.

Aides failed to realize that the six-foot Kentuckian's leg was bleeding profusely. A large artery just below their leader's knee joint had been severed, but little blood was immediately visible. As a result, Johnston bled to death without getting medical attention. Those who examined the body came to a reluctant conclusion. From the location and angle of the wound, it appeared likely that one of the Confederate leader's own men might have fired the accidental, fatal shot.

On May 8, 1862, the president of the United States was exposed to hostile gunfire for the first time. Aboard a steam tug, Abraham Lincoln was near Sewell's Point, eager for a firsthand look at the way in which riverboats could deal with Confederate shore batteries near Norfolk.

By using the USS *Monitor, Susquehanna,* and *E. A. Stevens,* the Federals hoped to make short work of land-based foes. As they steamed toward their objective, men aboard the *Stevens* were keenly aware that they were less than one mile behind the president. Careful to avoid hitting his tug, they elevated their Parrott gun to lob shells into the shore batteries.

Lincoln escaped without a scratch, but vessels that made up the little flotilla did not fare equally well. Men aboard the *Monitor* listened with horrified amazement as shrapnel from the *Stevens* screamed toward the ironclad. Some shells fired from the gunboat exploded prematurely and fell far short of their objectives on shore.

Aboard the *Susquehanna,* crew members saw a spanker take a direct hit from the rifled gun of their sister vessel. "Only an act of Providence saved Abraham Lincoln from a random shell fired by one of his own gunboats," a participant in the action concluded.

On June 1 opposing forces prepared for a brisk skirmish at Strasburg, Virginia. In predawn darkness, firing from the rear created a wild stampede by Confederates who fled from rain-soaked tents. Men of the Sixth Virginia Cavalry rushed through the camp of the Second Virginia Cavalry before the latter knew what was happening.

Continuing their hasty flight, some members of the Sixth Cavalry burst into a clearing occupied by men of the Seventh Louisiana Infantry. Busy cooking their breakfast, the startled members of the Louisiana force, sure that the enemy had caught them off guard, delivered a volley against the Virginia cavalrymen.

At Corinth, Mississippi, the general officer of the day of Brig. Gen. John Pope's army learned how suddenly friendly fire can erupt. Maj. Frank J. Jones of the Sixth Ohio Infantry noted in his journal that at daybreak "all was quiet."

Suddenly men throughout the Union force were horrified to receive word of another tragedy caused by some of their comrades. Describing the last hour of the victim, Jones wrote: "He was inspecting the picket line and testing the qualities of a soldier stationed at one of the most dangerous points. Notwithstanding the challenge given him, he continued to advance—and paid the penalty of his rashness by receiving a mortal wound at the hands of this faithful soldier. The officer was popular, and his death was deeply lamented."

A trio of memorable incidents near Malvern Hill, Virginia, occurred on July 1, 1862. When Federal gunboats on the James River opened fire, "all their shot landed in or close by a Union battery."

At Malvern Hill a member of the U.S. Signal Service was forced to send a message urging Federal troops to cease firing. [HARPER'S WEEKLY]

Describing the debacle later, Maj. Gen. Fitz-John Porter said that the accidental killing proceeded for some time. It stopped only when a member of the Signal Service flashed an urgent message to commanders of gunboats: "For God's sake stop firing."

Porter admitted that he never learned what took place as a result of one of his orders of the same day. At his direction, three batteries headed toward Crew's Hill with instructions to "join in the fight if necessary, but not to permit the advance of the foe, even if it must be arrested at the risk of firing upon friends."

By dusk, Confederate units were, if possible, in greater confusion than the Federals. Without authorization, one of Brig. Gen. John B. Magruder's officers went to the front to try to separate two brigades. Eventually he managed to station them almost a mile apart. Yet as light dimmed rapidly, forces commanded by Brig. Gen. Joseph B. Kershaw and Brig. Gen. Paul J. Semmes were fired upon, not from the enemy in front, but from the rear. How many of the five thousand dead and wounded were casualties of friendly fire, no commander dared estimate.

At Antietam, Federal forces forded a creek and were fired upon by their comrades. [HARPER'S HISTORY OF THE CIVIL WAR]

The largest single-day casualty list of the war occurred on September 17, 1862, part of which stemmed from an epidemic of friendly fire. Of the estimated twelve thousand men in blue who fell that day, about twenty-two hundred went down in a corn field near Antietam during a period of twenty minutes.

Federal officers never liked to admit that some men became so panic-stricken that they ran from their enemies. Survivors never wavered in their insistence that when this happened, Union gunners opened fire on chaotic masses in which many of their own colleagues were intermingled with temporarily victorious Confederates.

On the Joseph Poffenberger farm, about four hundred men were killed or wounded in a matter of minutes. Many of them were casualties of two volleys fired from Federal regiments. While trying to flank a stone wall, men of two units in blue thought they were facing the enemy, so they leveled their fire at one another.

Maj. Gen. Joseph K. Mansfield, who later received a mortal wound that day, was horrified at witnessing an action he was powerless to stop. Men of the Tenth Maine Infantry halted briefly in a field bordered by Smoketown Road. They spotted a band of soldiers scurrying for cover in the East Woods, so they quickly opened fire. Mansfield tried to order them to cease fire, but confusion was so great that the message never reached them. By the time the men from Maine had emptied their guns, those stragglers in blue who were not lying on the field had made it to safety in the woods.

At another center of chaotic action, men of the Fifty-ninth New York Infantry were told to stop a frontal assault by Confederates. Hastily reloading their guns and without having had a signal, they fired almost in concert—directly into the backs of the men of the Fifteenth Maine Infantry. Col. John W. Kimball of the target regiment raced to the side of Maj. Gen. Edwin V. Sumner. "For God's sake," he reputedly shouted to his commander, "tell the New Yorkers to cease fire; they're killing your men as fast as the enemy!"

On the Mumma farm during the same day's action, men of the Fourteenth Connecticut Infantry halted briefly near the edge of another corn field. A picket spotted men running toward them, so a spontaneous but ragged volley was fired. Only when men in advance of the rest reached the line of soldiers in blue did the Connecticut troops learn that they had cut down comrades under the command of Brig. Gen. Max Weber.

Even veteran soldiers manning some Union batteries added to casualties caused by friendly fire that day at Antietam. With darkness rapidly approaching, gunners of a Maryland battery decided to get off a few more shots. Seeking to fire over the heads of troops making up a regiment from Maine, they underestimated the range. As a result, their first round took out four Federals, and their second knocked a lieutenant from his horse.

Barely halfway through the war, the toll from friendly fire was mounting rapidly. Instead of abating, it plagued combat units on both sides for another eighteen months. Irwinville, Georgia, was the site of the last documented instance.

On May 10, 1865, scattered forces led by Brig. Gen. James H. Wilson converged on a party of fleeing Southerners who included Jefferson Davis. With the capture of the Confederate president only minutes away, cavalrymen in blue were in a fever of excitement.

Men of two regiments found what they believed to be clues and raced toward them independently. As they approached their target they opened fire, not upon Confederates, but upon one another. In this final instance of fatal friendly fire, two Federal riders died and a number of their comrades were wounded.

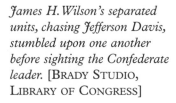

James H. Wilson's separated units, chasing Jefferson Davis, stumbled upon one another before sighting the Confederate leader. [BRADY STUDIO, LIBRARY OF CONGRESS]

Probably the most famous instance of friendly fire occurred in May 1863 near the hamlet of Chancellorsville, Virginia. A single shot by a soldier in gray may have been one of the most decisive of the millions of shots fired during the war.

Lt. Gen. Thomas J. "Stonewall" Jackson was executing Robert E. Lee's audacious plan that led to a stunning Confederate victory on May 4, 1863. With the attack having started late in the afternoon of May 2, Jackson and several of his staff had ridden out between the lines to reconnoiter that night. The lines between the two armies, however, were not clearly delineated, and with reports that Union cavalry were patrolling the woods, a North Carolina unit opened fire on a cluster of riders moving toward them. A single ball shattered Jackson's left arm. The arm was amputated, but the general developed pneumonia while he was being removed from the area as a consequence of his wound. The man whom Lee called his "strong right arm" died a short week later, the most celebrated and important victim of Civil War friendly fire.

CHAPTER

3

Accidentally On Purpose

Men under the command of Brig. Gen. Nathaniel Lyon swore never to forget that he ordered them to fire on civilians during a Saint Louis riot. Although friends and relatives of those who were killed donned blue because they loved the Union, they admitted they'd like to see Lyon dead.

Haters of the commander had plenty of opportunities to act during chaotic fighting at Wilson's Creek, Missouri, in August 1861. When the career military officer dropped from his saddle, dead before he hit the ground, it was impossible to know who had fired the fatal bullet. A rumor, undocumented but widespread, suggested that the battle had provided an opportunity for one of his men to settle an old score.

Despite the fact that a man put his life on the line when he wrote about execution-style killings, some clear-cut reports were penned. Although an older term than friendly fire, fragging had not yet entered general use at war's end. Regardless of what it was called, there is no question that it flourished.

Hatred of callous and brutal commanders was behind many a sudden death. Others stemmed from resentment at unit reorganizations. This often occurred when a regiment or a brigade was overmanned while others had not met their quotas. Men shifted into strange units under officers for whom they had not voted were prone to respond with challenges or violence.

Some fractious words that were never translated into fatal action were too serious to be ignored. Strangely, many more threats and murders from within the victim's command show up in Federal letters and diaries than in Confederate sources.

Tempers were on edge among men of the Seventy-ninth New York Infantry after the battle of Bull Run. Out of three hundred officers and men in its ranks, at least sixty did not survive the first battle of the war. Comprised largely of soldiers who were proud of their Scottish blood, the regiment suffered what even U.S. Secretary of War Simon Cameron labeled as an abuse of power.

Hoping to soothe frayed feelings, Washington instructed the unit's acting commander, Lt. Col. Samuel M. Elliott, to prepare for an election of a new commanding officer. It was imperative, he was told, to replace Col. James Cameron, a casualty of the Manassas fray. As in many Federal units, the top staff officer of the Seventy-ninth would be chosen, not by a vote among the ranks, but by a conclave of commissioned officers.

With the election set for the afternoon of August 13, 1861, enlisted men grumbled louder than ever. Many of them declared that they'd serve under no colonel unless he was properly elected.

Seventy-two hours before the all-important election, Col. Isaac Stevens arrived at the camp and took command. Papers showed that he had been appointed from Washington on July 30. A West Point graduate and veteran of the Mexican War, he immediately made it clear that he was a spit-and-polish professional soldier who would tolerate no nonsense.

Six officers, including Maj. David McClellan and Capt. Thomas Barclay, resigned when Stevens took charge. At dress parade following their departure, the men of the regiment were told by Stevens that they must move their camp to Maryland immediately. Their anger was exacerbated by their having earlier received an unauthorized promise that they would be sent to New York City for reorganization.

Before dawn on August 14, three-fourths of the regiment had vowed that they would obey no order from Stevens. When he instructed the men to strike their tents, they stood motionless and jeered at him. Furious, the new colonel directed officers to do the job, preparatory to moving.

As junior officers stalked through the camp knocking supports from tents, a private lifted a loaded musket and pointed it at Lt. William Lusk, muttering, "It was appointed for at least one officer to die." Just as he pulled the trigger, a comrade knocked the weapon upward and away from the officer. Lusk, who wrote home about the incident, would have been the first documented victim of fragging had his foe's shot gone as intended.

A camp incident such as that which took place in the ranks of the Seventy-ninth New York was rare. One week prior to this dramatic near miss, Federals under Bvt. Col. E. R. S. Canby of the Tenth Infantry had clashed with retreating Confederates.

According to the *Rebellion Record,* the opposing forces met near Santa Fe, New Mexico. "A battle ensued, in which the rebels were routed. Col. Sibley [possibly misnamed by newspaper correspondents familiar with Federal Col. C. C. Sibley] was assassinated by his own men, who charged him with drunkenness and inefficiency."

On January 14, 1862, the *Cincinnati Gazette* reprinted a letter that had appeared earlier in the *Louisville Courier.* According to it, men making up the Irish Tigers from New Orleans nearly rebelled when two of their number were shot "for some trifling military offense."

The letter writer, who didn't dare attach his name to his report, continued: "As a sequel to the execution of the two 'Tigers,' by order of court-martial, I have to record that, yesterday morning, *the bodies of two officers of the Seventh Louisiana regiment were found with their throats cut.* They were the officers of the day and of the guard, at the time of the commission of disrespect by the 'Tigers,' and were instrumental in bringing them to punishment."

On March 1 the *Pittsburgh Chronicle* published a detailed account from a local soldier. Having frequently been in close contact with captured Confederates, said the writer, he was confident of a Federal victory very soon. This stemmed in part, he wrote, from the fact that "Gen. [Leonidas] Polk has not the confidence of a single man in the army. He swears like a trooper, and in case of a fight he will be the first to be shot, and by his own soldiers."

With Federal forces on the attack, former U.S. Secretary of War John B. Floyd was in command at Fort Donelson in Tennessee. Without notice, the man who was now a prominent Confederate turned his command over to Brig. Gen. Simon Buckner and made his escape, leaving Buckner to be forced into unconditional surrender by Brig. Gen. U. S. Grant.

Reporting the fashion in which the former cabinet member had saved his own skin, the *New York Times* reported, "The feeling was so strong against Floyd, that several of the confederate soldiers

At Fort Donelson, combatants found that the woods and swamps did not allow classic European battlefield tactics. [THE SOLDIER IN OUR CIVIL WAR]

fired at him as he was leaving, and it is asserted by many that he was killed."

News of Floyd's death at the hands of his own men was premature. On March 11, Jefferson Davis relieved from command the reported target and transferred him into the Virginia militia.

Fighting in the Shenandoah Valley under the leadership of Stonewall Jackson, Brig. Gen. C. S. Winder was said to be targeted for death by his own men. He punished soldiers right and left, once ordering thirty of them to be bucked and gagged simultaneously.

This punishment, commonly inflicted by both sides, was seldom life-threatening. A culprit was gagged, usually by having a stick pushed into his mouth. With hands and feet tied while he was sitting on the ground with knees drawn between his arms, he had a tree limb inserted over his arms and under his knees.

"This fellow won't ride away from our next battle," Winder's men whispered to one another. In spite of this rumor, the general survived both the Valley campaign and the Seven Days. At the start of the Cedar Mountain action, he was so sick that he went into battle in an ambulance. Official reports say he was killed by Federal artillery on August 7, 1862. Veterans who had served under him were never positive that this account of his death was accurate.

Col. Thomas T. Heath of the Fifth Ohio Cavalry received a new recruit late in July 1862. Calling himself Bully Butcher Boy, the new member of the regiment soon found himself punished by buck and gag.

Unable to form words, Bully Butcher Boy fumed and snorted while forced to remain motionless for hours in front of his new comrades. As soon as he was released from his punishment, he rushed behind his colonel's back and mouthed a silent promise: "First time we get into the smoke, Little Colonel, I'll empty your saddle!"

Though Heath survived the war, he did not forget the incident from which he learned never to turn his back upon his men during battle.

Educated men in the ranks of the Fifth Iowa Infantry described Col. W. H. Worthington as "a military martinet." In September 1862 the officer, who knew most of his men hated him, scouted an enemy position and then started back to his own lines. A picket stationed behind a tree saw him coming, stepped into the clear, and fired a bullet that struck the colonel in the middle of his forehead.

Arrested and tried, the killer was acquitted but the verdict convinced only a minority of men in the regiment. Many of them wrote home about the incident, stressing their conviction that Worthington—who had received many threats—had been murdered in cold blood.

About the time Worthington died, Federal Brig. Gen. William "Bull" Nelson was the subject of a plot. His nickname grew out of the way he roared orders and obscenities to his men. Described as having "an imperious temper, demoniac energy, and brutal man-

Brig. Gen. Jefferson C. Davis murdered Brig. Gen. William "Bull" Nelson in a Louisville hotel. [HARPER'S WEEKLY]

ners," he boasted that he once "personally cut down some Union men who fought badly."

Many of the men in his command were Hoosiers who had known each other since boyhood. According to the *Cincinnati Enquirer,* they banded together and swore to kill Nelson the next time they went into battle.

Nelson, however, did not take a bullet in the back. Brig. Gen. Jefferson C. Davis, a subordinate with a fiery temper who had grown up in Indiana, quarreled with the intemperate Nelson in public. On the day before Union troops were scheduled to march south, Davis murdered Nelson in a Louisville hotel.

Brig. Gen. Thomas Wilson, a native of New York who grew up in Michigan, entered the U.S. Army after graduating from West Point in 1837. Professional soldiers learned to live under his dictatorial leadership, but the volunteers whom he commanded from 1861 to 1862 did not.

While posted in North Carolina, he twice fell into carefully prepared traps that his men labeled "pitfalls." After having quarreled

Gen. Frank P. Blair Jr. contributed to conditions that led to an explosion of violence in the streets of Saint Louis. [NICOLAY AND HAY, ABRAHAM LINCOLN]

with many of his officers, he was transferred to the West. During the August 5, 1862, battle of Baton Rouge, Williams died in action.

A widely circulated story, never documented, asserts that he was killed by artillery rather than by small-arms fire. According to this account, the tyrannical brigadier was seized by a group of his own men, who held him in front of a cannon, before signaling for it to be fired at the enemy.

Confederate Brig. Gen. Thomas R. R. Cobb acquired a reputation as an abuser of his soldiers during the Seven Days and at Second Bull Run in July and August 1862. He led his brigade to Fredericksburg, where he died under strange circumstances on December 13. Oral tradition asserts that there was no doubt that he was shot from behind by one or more of his own men.

Union Maj. Gen. Frank P. Blair Jr., brother of a member of Lincoln's cabinet, was widely blamed for murders in the streets of Saint Louis. Although he was not present when Nathaniel Lyon's men cut down civilians on those streets, the evidence supports the view that his policies helped to create the crisis that led to the riot.

Some soldiers in blue, though devoted to the Union, never forgave Blair for his role in the mass tragedy. As a division commander in the Seventeenth Corps during the Atlanta campaign, he realized that he was the subject of pent-up anger.

Recalling that period, Capt. Chester G. Higbee of the Twelfth Wisconsin Infantry later wrote: "Finally, a man (I think from the Sixteenth Wisconsin) fired at the general in open daylight and was arrested and it was said by the guards that the soldier frankly told General Blair that he intended to kill him. This ill-feeling was so general that I have often wondered why General Blair continued in command of that corps."

Six feet tall and inordinately proud of the number of horses killed under him, George A. Custer became a brigadier general at the age of twenty-three. His promotion meant that numerous older men who considered him a stranger were forced to serve under him.

Custer stripped some officers of their rank, ordered one to a court-martial, and sent culprits to the gallows on the slightest provocation. As a result, men he dubbed "western ruffians" came close to staging a mutiny.

Custer pretended to be oblivious of the dissidence; not so his wife, Libby. According to her, a stream of threats came to their home. Staff members, whose tents were pitched on the lawn before the Custer home, "tried to persuade the general to lock the doors and bolt the windows." Custer survived the war but went down at the Little Big Horn in 1876 at the hands of Native Americans.

At least one Union officer reversed the usual pattern of fragging by killing a subordinate. A sergeant of a Pennsylvania regiment reputedly defied Col. Samuel P. Spear of the Eleventh Pennsylvania Cavalry. "Damn you," he's believed to have told the colonel, "you have drafted us, but you can't make us fight."

Hours after the verbal clash, Spear shot and killed the rebellious sergeant without the presence of witnesses. When charged by the *Wilkes-Barre Union* with having murdered a subordinate, Spear refused to comment.

Even an enlisted man was not immune from the danger that a comrade would treat him as though he were a member of an enemy force.

George A. Custer received his first general's stars at the age of twenty-three. [NATIONAL ARCHIVES]

Pvts. John Rowley and Jerome Dupoy of the Seventh Connecticut Infantry quarreled, then fought with knives. Dupoy got the better of his comrade and left him with a series of deep flesh wounds.

Rowley put his knife aside but swore that he'd find a chance to get revenge. It came during the February 1864 battle of Olustee, Florida. When Dupoy was killed instantly by a single shot in the head, a court-martial was convened. Through its verdict, Rowley became the only man known to have been executed for having killed a member of his own company.

Brig. Gen. Jefferson C. Davis, the unpunished killer of Brig. Gen. William Nelson, commanded the Seventeenth Corps during Sherman's march from Atlanta to Savannah. Near the coast, Davis was forced to build a pontoon bridge to get his men across Ebenezer Creek. Once over, he destroyed the bridge to prevent escaped slaves, or contrabands, from continuing to follow his force.

Dr. James C. Patten, a corps surgeon, labeled these actions of his commander as "dastardly." To his journal he confided that he'd have Davis hanged if he had the power to do so. He ended his account of the matter by saying: "There is great indignation among the troops. I should not wonder if the valiant murderer of women and children should meet with an accident before long." The expectations—or hopes—of Patten were never realized; Davis survived until 1879.

According to Sgt. Maj. H. W. Manson of Dale's Confederate Sharpshooters, an unidentified Federal was unfortunate. At what Manson called "point blank range of less than forty steps," he saw "a tall, angular Federal" fall when he turned a Sharpe's rifle upon him.

Two days later, a wounded prisoner walked into a hospital tent where the Confederate was working temporarily. He instantly recognized the man he had dropped and found that his ball had hit his opponent's collarbone. To his surprise, though, the most visible wound was near the back of the jaw of the soldier in blue.

Questioned, he tried to seem casual as he explained to Manson that after having been knocked down by the Confederate rifle ball, "Some of our own cowardly fellows shot me in the jaw when I got up."

Logic asserts that for every instance of fragging reported, there must have been many more similar incidents. From private to brigadier general, few on either side of the conflict were 100 percent sure they wouldn't be dropped by calculated fire from a comrade in arms.

4

Things That Couldn't Be Counted

After every battle, commanders wanted a reasonably accurate casualty count, an all-important matter in an official report. Since there was no way to ascertain the number of opposing soldiers who had been wounded, many generals employed a formula. They multiplied the known dead by six or seven to estimate the total casualties in an opposing force.

Naturally, most or all leaders of armies, corps, and brigades tried to minimize their own losses and magnify the losses of the enemy. Accuracy could be attained only by a tally of rosters in a given command, and this activity was seldom pursued in the aftermath of a major battle.

Arms, legs, heads, and other body parts were all-important to men who lost them, but they are rarely mentioned in military records. Letters, diaries, and memoirs are the only significant sources of information about these things that were of monumental significance to those who left them behind.

Enemy fire consistently severed arms, legs, and heads, not only from bodies of soldiers, but also from their mounts. William W. Loring spent much of the war as a Confederate brigadier, functioning with only one arm—he had left the other about three miles from Mexico City. A spent bullet knocked him unconscious in the September 12, 1847, battle of Chapultepec, so he always joked that he got off lightly, as he might have lost his head instead of his arm.

Irish-born Thomas Sweeny marched off to Mexico with the First New York Volunteers. In the 1848 battle of Churubusco he lost his

The dead were counted after all engagements to estimate total casualties.
[LIBRARY OF CONGRESS]

right arm. Habitually keeping his empty right sleeve folded, the professional soldier reached the rank of captain on January 19, 1861, and just four months later became a Federal brigadier.

After every major battle, surgeons went to work with saws. More often than not, huge piles of severed limbs accumulated wherever they worked.

At Gettysburg, Federal medical officers were more meticulous than usual. They dumped amputated limbs into big barrels that were buried soon after they were filled. Months later, when decomposition of flesh was complete, the barrels were dug up and sent to the medical college in Washington. Used in teaching, these bones meant that many a veteran contributed to a doctor's education without knowing about it.

Inevitably, the conflict produced tens of thousands of severed body parts that disappeared without a trace. In a few instances, something

Amputees were often placed under the comforting shade of trees to regain consciousness. [NATIONAL ARCHIVES]

is known about these byproducts of battle—with hair dominating the record.

Members of the Twelfth Mississippi Infantry were too late to be able to brag about helping to win a smashing victory at Bull Run. Members of the regiment spent the night of Sunday, July 21, traveling between Lynchburg and Manassas, Virginia. They didn't reach Manassas Junction until the first big encounter of the war was over.

One member of the unit, Pvt. T. G. Dabney, never tired of telling how astonished he was when he reached the field of battle. "We jumped off our train near a cluster of little shacks that were being used as field hospitals," he recalled. "It was impossible for a fellow who had never been in conflict to take his eyes off bloody dismembered limbs that had accumulated in huge piles."

On the second day at Gettysburg, Union Maj. Gen. Daniel E. Sickles took a direct hit from a Confederate shell. Within thirty minutes a surgeon had finished amputating his mangled leg.

Sickles loudly demanded that it be preserved in alcohol, but he soon became tired of it and donated it to the U.S. Army Medical Museum. Tradition says he visited his leg several times during the postwar years but never remained with it more than a few minutes.

At Stones River Pvt. John Long achieved distinction, of a sort. Confederate iron and lead mangled one of his legs so that there was no hope it could be saved. Unwilling to wait for a surgeon to act, the wounded man in blue pulled out his pocketknife and went to work. Long is the only soldier positively known to have amputated what remained of his own leg.

During the battle of Port Hudson, a round from a Union battery blew off the leg of Capt. R. M. Boone. Aware that he had only a few minutes to live, the Confederate artillery officer made a dying request. Records do not indicate whether or not men of his battery complied with it. His last wish, he said, was to have his severed leg stuffed into one of his guns and shot toward the enemy.

Union Col. Ulric Dahlgren, who was killed in the Kilpatrick-Dahlgren raid on Richmond, had earlier acquired a splendid wooden leg. After his death the artificial limb went on display in the window of a department store in the Confederate capital.

It stayed there only briefly, however. Confederate Lt. James Pollard, head of the unit that ambushed Dahlgren, soon lost his own leg. He claimed Dahlgren's as a prize of war and tried to have it fitted for him. Finding that he couldn't use that piece of Federal wood himself, Pollard gave the leg to amputee John N. Ballard, who wore it for the duration of the war.

Struck by a Union shell at Brandy Station, Confederate Capt. William Farley was soon found by a rescue squad whose members made ready to take him to a field hospital. As he was lifted upon the litter, Farley gestured vigorously and with all the breath he could muster made a poignant plea: "Don't leave my leg lying in this pasture," he implored. "Hand it to me, so I can take it with me."

During the Confederate retreat from Nashville in 1863, a gun was accidentally discharged. The shot hit a Private Allen of the Thirty-sixth Alabama Infantry with such force that the only hope of saving his life lay in immediate amputation.

Artist Alfred Waud was photographed while sketching at Gettysburg. [BRADY STUDIO, LIBRARY OF CONGRESS]

Chaplain L. M. Hutton agreed to remain with the soldier after the hasty surgery. Soon the pair of stragglers were captured by a Federal unit.

Recalling the memorable day, Hutton said that as soon as he saw the bluecoats coming, his first act was to bury Allen's leg. He didn't have time, however, to erect for it even a crude wooden marker of the sort often used on battlefields.

Near Adairsville, Georgia, Federal surgeons established a field hospital in the loft of what had once been a fine brick store. They treated a few wounded Confederates as well as their own men, with surgery being the most common procedure. Upon evacuating the impromptu surgical theater, they were charged with having buried severed limbs of Union soldiers while deliberately leaving behind "the amputated leg of an unfortunate rebel."

Alfred R. Waud, a native of England, is believed to have executed more Civil War sketches than any other artist during the war. In

1862 he moved from the *New York Illustrated News* to *Harper's Weekly,* whose readers quickly came to look for his signature. Waud followed the Army of the Potomac in all of its major campaigns and often sent to New York sketches of everyday events in the lives of soldiers.

At an unidentified field hospital the artist saw surgeons at work, using the stump of a big tree as an operating table. A man whose right leg had just been amputated was being taken away on a stretcher.

Editors frequently lauded Waud for the accuracy of his work. This time, however, they considered him to have been too meticulous. Readers would be appalled at the horrors of war if his surgical sketch should be published as he submitted it, the management decided.

Unwilling to discard a vivid illustration, staff artists were told to turn the wounded man around so that the stump of his leg wouldn't be seen. It was this revised version that was published for wartime viewing. Yet the original piece of art, with the bandaged stump of a leg clearly visible, eventually found a home. It is preserved in the Library of Congress.

Arms were probably severed from bodies even more frequently than legs. Sometimes action took place with no surgery involved. After the battle of Antietam, a survivor proudly discussed the deadly work done by guns of Federal Battery B.

Every time a cannon roared, he said, the gunner's aim was so precise that debris briefly filled the air. Ripped haversacks and broken handguns became almost commonplace as they rose, then dropped back to the ground. In one instance, recalled the Union gunner, "A severed arm still covered with a gray sleeve shot 30 feet into the air before it gently spiralled back toward the point at which the fellow who once relied upon it was lying upon his back."

Also at Antietam, Lt. Ezra E. Stickley of the Fifth Virginia Infantry suffered irreparable losses. When recuperating from injuries, he bemoaned having left behind a splendid horse and all of his personal belongings. Even worse, he said, when brigade surgeons took off his mangled right arm they casually tossed it under a kitchen table instead of saving it for him.

By far the most notable of severed limbs once went into battle by the side of Stonewall Jackson. At Chancellorsville, when he was hit in the left arm by fire from his own men, the wound required the

The editors of Harper's Weekly *refused to publish this Alfred Waud sketch until the amputee's position was reversed.* [HARPER'S WEEKLY]

arm's amputation. Had complications not developed, however, he might have survived the battlefield injury.

After Jackson's death, relatives and admirers saw to it that his severed left arm was given a respectful burial in the graveyard of the Lacy family near Chancellorsville. Soon a gravestone—believed to be the only one of its kind—was erected to mark the last resting place of Jackson's arm.

Hair, whether from the head of a combat victim or not, was valued as a souvenir. That's why the Louisiana Historical Association was glad to receive the gift of an envelope containing hair from the head of Jefferson Davis.

Headed for the gallows, convicted spy Marcellus Clarke (who frequently disguised himself as "Sue Mundy") borrowed a knife from a guard. When he had carefully severed a big hank of his hair, he made the "last request customarily afforded to a man about to die." The hair, he instructed, should be transmitted to men who made up the raiding company he once commanded "and carefully divided among them."

In a gesture of quite different nature, partisan raider John S. Mosby once cut off a lock of hair. Packaged for transmission along with a letter, he dispatched it to the White House in Washington.

There's no certainty that Abraham Lincoln ever saw the Confederate hair sent to him to emphasize threats that the president was likely soon to have his head shaved as a preliminary to his execution.

Richard Slade, a private who fought in gray, rejoiced at his good fortune. During a furious battle he received a direct hit but was uninjured except for a shattered left hand.

Writing to his loved ones, Slade told them of his injury and added: "It looks hard to see them take off legs & arms & cut men into pieces—but thank God, they got only a little part of me."

Jesse James, who fought briefly as a Confederate partisan, managed to dodge Federal bullets. Probably while engaged in target practice, he clipped off the end of one of his fingers. Though the body part involved was tiny, it eventually proved to be important. That missing fingertip was vital to identification of James's body when he was murdered in 1880.

Union forces involved in an early expedition aimed at coastal installations in North Carolina had never "seen the elephant," a phrase meaning that one had been in combat. An amphibious force that landed in near darkness spent the night without shelter and the next morning marched toward a Confederate fort.

When the Southerners' big guns began to boom, men in blue fell right and left. One of them, an unnamed captain, was apparently uninjured except that he lost his head when he fell.

Awed comrades, surveying the headless body of their friend, wondered what had happened. They eventually agreed that a cannon ball had created so strong a wind that it decapitated the man whose head it barely missed.

In Kansas, one of William C. Quantrill's raiders was so ruthless that he became known as Bloody Bill Anderson. After having formed his own band of partisans, he frequently led them into Missouri.

Near the hamlet of Orrick, he failed to realize that Union forces were waiting to ambush him. As soon as he came within range of their guns, his body was riddled with lead.

Victorious Federal soldiers dumped the body of the guerrilla fighter into a cart and hauled it to the village of Richmond, Missouri. They triumphantly mounted Bloody Bill's severed head on the highest telegraph pole in the area.

Anderson's one-time commander was treated with even less respect. After Confederate reverses in 1864, Quantrill set out for Washington with the avowed purpose of assassinating Lincoln.

He never came close to fulfilling his objective. While hiding out in Kentucky he was discovered by Federal troops and wounded. Quantrill died of his wounds three weeks later on June 6, 1865, in a prison hospital. He was buried in an unmarked grave. Logically, that should have ended his movements—but it did not.

Years later, biographer Albert Castel learned that twelve years after Quantrill's death the guerrilla leader's mother received permission to move the remains to a family cemetery. For this undertaking she enlisted the aid of William C. Scott, a long-time friend.

Believing himself to have been handed a bonanza, Scott stole Quantrill's skull and several bones from his arms and legs. They didn't attract the interest he expected and no one offered a fancy price for the relics. As a result, the bones of the Kansas border ruffian eventually went to the state historical society in Topeka. Quantrill's skull didn't accompany them, however. For reasons unknown, it wound up in the collection of the Dover Historical Society in Delaware.

More than thirty years after the hostilities ended, the Louisiana Historical Society published a list of relics presented to it by twenty-three donors during a period of just three months.

Among the 130 items with which private owners parted was a gift from Mrs. Charles L. Ball of Saint Louis. Because of "its historical significance," she somewhat reluctantly sent to the society "a lock of hair of Gen. [Felix K.] Zollicoffer, clipped by her father while the General's body was in the hands of the Federals, who killed him."

*The head of Gen. George G.
Meade's horse, Baldy, was
preserved and honored in
Philadelphia after the death
of its master.* [LIBRARY OF
CONGRESS]

Another item in the same inventory came from Mrs. W. H.
Adams. She described it as "one iron fork, with handle made from
the bone of a dead Federal soldier." According to the donor, this
trophy was given to Pat Barrow, her father, during his 1863 imprisonment in New Orleans.

At least one famous animal contributed to the small store of body
parts about which we know at least a little. After the battle of Bull
Run, a captain in the Federal Topographical Engineers bought a
wounded horse that he named Baldy.

Baldy took his owner to Fredericksburg and Chancellorsville, then
to Pennsylvania and Gettysburg. He survived his master by a few
years, and at his death executors of the estate of Maj. Gen. George
G. Meade had the horse's head mounted—complete with mane.

Eventually presented to Philadelphia's War Library and
Museum, the head of Meade's horse became a fixture at meetings
of the Civil War Round Table in the City of Brotherly Love.

Quantrill's skull, Sickles's leg, and Jackson's arm, collectively, fall
far short of the importance of one small collection of body parts.
Dried drops of blood, tiny fragments of bone, and bits of tissue

After Lincoln had been shot in Ford's Theater, tiny fragments of his tissue were preserved. [HARPER'S WEEKLY]

make up this treasure trove. It represents samples salvaged from the body of Abraham Lincoln before he was prepared for burial.

Small as they are, these specimens have potential for unlocking a major riddle. By subjecting them to DNA tests, it is believed possible to learn whether or not the president was afflicted with Marfan syndrome. This condition causes elongation of arms and legs, often affects the heart, and can lead to early death. Because of the president's physical appearance, Lincoln may have been afflicted with the syndrome and might have had a very short life expectancy at the time he was assassinated.

Custodians of these bits and pieces that represent all that remain of Abraham Lincoln's body have so far refused to permit them to be tested. They may hold the solution to a puzzle that may never be solved.

Part Two

Things Change

Life was relatively stable, almost static, when Alfred Lord Tennyson penned his "Locksley Hall." Yet even in that placid era he foretold: "Let the great world spin forever down the ringing grooves of change." Until the dawn of the electronic age, no period saw America and Americans change as rapidly as during the approximately fourteen hundred days of civil war. It would almost seem that earlier generations had been hoarding energy that would bring about innovations and launch inventions. War released this pent-up store in such fashion that a torrent of change became a distinguishing mark of the period.

The bombardment of Fort Sumter touched off a revolution that affected every aspect of life in America. [HARPER'S HISTORY OF THE CIVIL WAR]

CHAPTER

5

Down the Ringing Grooves of Change

Seven months after Confederates fired upon Fort Sumter, a headline in Horace Greeley's *New York Herald* proclaimed: THE GREAT REBELLION A GREAT REVOLUTION. Taking the long view, an editorial suggested, "Everything the finger of war touches is revolutionized." Even a hasty glance at a few areas of life—civilian as well as military—indicates that the statement was accurate.

Wandering from his native New York to the West, Gail Borden invented what he called a "meat biscuit" in 1851. Two years later he devised a way to reduce the bulk and increase the shelf life of milk. His 1856 patent for condensed milk evoked little or no interest; however, it is worth noting in April 1861 that Capt. Gustavus V. Fox included air-dried or "desiccated" food in his attempt to resupply Fort Sumter.

More than seventy-five thousand volunteers answered Lincoln's call for troops. Yet once they began to assemble, it became obvious that standard kitchen practices would be inadequate. Within months Borden's 1856 patent took on an importance beyond anything the inventor had envisioned. Anticipating an enormous demand, he opened a large "condensary" at Wassaic, New York.

Although initial interest was not as great as Borden had anticipated, following the September 1862 battle at Antietam, the U.S. Sanitary Commission initiated an order for twenty-six hundred pounds. At the May 1863 battle of Chancellorsville, Robert E. Lee sent a supply of condensed milk and whiskey for the relief of wounded men in blue who were lying on the field and starving. By

Gail Borden invented a "meat biscuit" in 1851 but found no market for it until 1861. [THE BORDEN COMPANY]

the time the conflict was three years old, inmates of Richmond's Libby Prison regarded Borden's product as a necessity.

Hundreds of thousands of soldiers were introduced to condensed milk during the conflict. Once veterans shed their uniforms, the innovation adopted as a military necessity became a staple in civilian life.

Footwear was as vital to both armies as condensed milk and other long-life foods. Members of infantry regiments who were continually on the march wore out shoes faster than new ones could be manufactured. Men fighting under Irvin McDowell, George B. McClellan, Ambrose Burnside, and other Union commanders had to have shoes to take the field against Confederates.

In 1860 an estimated 12,500 establishments made shoes; collectively they employed at least 120,000 workmen. At the time, a skilled cobbler could handcraft three pairs of shoes per day. Forced by necessity to change, the shoe industry abandoned traditional hand manufacture in small shops. Large buildings with lofts and abandoned cotton mills were equipped with stitching machines—power equipment that had been perfected by Lyman R. Blake in

1858 but had seen little use. Once war broke out, Blake's invention became of crucial importance in the North.

Mass produced under the leadership of Gordon McKay, the Blake invention was offered on generous terms. Any shoe manufacturer could modernize his shop for a down payment of five hundred dollars and a royalty of five cents for every pair of shoes stitched. Soon the average worker was turning out six or more pairs of shoes a day. As a result of this radical change in the industrial sector, most soldiers in blue remained well shod after thousands of their foes were forced to go barefoot because they had no shoes.

Clothing manufacturing was transformed within months after the conflict began. With seventy-five thousand men involved in the first Federal call for volunteers, the U.S. War Department had on hand a stock of clothing for only thirteen thousand soldiers.

Especially in Massachusetts, production of woolen uniforms literally exploded. At Lawrence, stockholders put about $2.5 million into buildings and machinery with which to enter this new field. Wartime dividends from this investment exceeded $3 million and the capital value of the original plant exceeded several times the 1861 figure.

Publisher Erastus Beadle envisioned a vast new market among common soldiers who often spent weeks in camp. Aided by editor Orville J. Victor, he printed and distributed enormous quantities of dime novels about such characters as Dick Turpin and Red Rover. Today's paperbacks are lineal descendants of Civil War "yellow backs," as they were widely called.

Aboard the USS *Connecticut,* Cmdr. Maxwell Woodhull was faced with the problem of providing well-balanced meals for his men. Fresh beef was needed in huge quantities, so he reluctantly consented to let junior officers resort to a novel technique.

On October 4, 1861, Woodhull reported to U.S. Secretary of the Navy Gideon Welles concerning the innovation developed aboard his ship: "Doubtless you are aware the plan for preserving beef was a new and entirely untried one, on the grand scale attempted in this vessel. It consisted of what is called an ice and chill room, something in the style of a refrigerator on shore. I did not approve of it from the very first moment I saw it. I saw nothing but a great consumer of ice, without the corresponding amount of cold element promised from it. There were 400 quarters of beef hung on hooks and stowed together as close as possible. I did not believe that the cold air, even if ever so abundant, could penetrate the mass sufficiently to preserve it."

Having found himself to be wrong, Woodhull noted that the ice room worked wonders in preserving the ship's beef. The discovery was doubly significant in that the *Connecticut* was on station in Florida waters. Once the experiment became common knowledge, rooms refrigerated with ice were set up in every Northern city.

The spiraling cost of the war created a fiscal crisis. There was not enough gold and silver in circulation to permit the free flow of commerce while military contracts were soaring in number and size.

U.S. Secretary of the Treasury Salmon P. Chase championed a radical change. Non-interest-bearing government notes were issued to serve as a medium of exchange in lieu of "hard money," or specie. Because they were printed in green ink on one side of the paper, these special war-issue notes were called "greenbacks."

Public opposition to the use of greenbacks was tremendous when they entered circulation. As a result, they depreciated in value and sometimes were traded at a rate of forty cents in gold or silver for a one-dollar greenback. Paper money with a face value of $450 million went into circulation as a result of a series of issues.

Late in 1865, with the war over, legislation was enacted to retire the greenbacks from circulation. Once the plan was initiated, a tremendous howl of public protest echoed throughout the land. People had become accustomed to paper currency and had decided that they liked it. As a result, legal tender issued during a wartime emergency became standard in the United States.

Although civilian life changed swiftly and radically, the pace of change in military matters was faster and more sweeping. Nevertheless, numerous high-ranking Union leaders looked askance at new-fangled rifles. These weapons were more accurate than muskets, they conceded, yet their wholesale use was not easily approved. Rifles used ammunition too rapidly to suit purchasing agents.

Oliver F. Winchester of Massachusetts didn't intend to go into the manufacture of military rifles, despite the fact that the long-time manufacturer of men's clothing became president of the New

Haven Arms Company in 1857. His firm produced fine sporting rifles for a wealthy clientele.

Tyler Henry, superintendent of the Winchester's arms manufacturing company, experimented successfully with rim-fire copper cartridges. At the U.S. War Department the new Henry rifle was not widely recommended, but thousands of individual Federal soldiers armed themselves with it at their own expense.

By war's end, the long-cherished musket was completely obsolete. Spurred by the success of Henry's weapon, Winchester began producing rifles in large quantities. As an indirect result of the Civil War, it was the new Winchester that came to be known as the rifle that tamed the West.

Coffee was high on the list of supplies most in demand by soldiers. Many Confederates were quickly forced to adopt crude substitutes, but Union soldiers insisted on the real thing.

Northern stockpiles of coffee beans were usually adequate to meet the demand, but many commanders balked at letting their men carry the bulky commodity. Wholesale merchants in a major port city, probably Philadelphia, devised what they considered to be a solution to the coffee problem.

Beans were ground to a fine powder, then mixed with sugar and milk to form a thick paste. Easily portable and not prone to spoil, a spoonful of paste and a cup of hot water generated a cup of coffee that a thirsty soldier would drink eagerly. Few civilians would today willingly down the brew, but it was this paste that presaged all modern forms of instant—or dehydrated—coffee.

It is acknowledged that naval warfare was suddenly and permanently altered as a result of an artillery duel between two vessels. Both the Federal *Monitor* and the Confederate *Virginia* (or *Merrimac*) were equipped with thick coats of iron. Their clash at Hampton Roads, Virginia, made wooden warships instantly obsolete; the Civil War innovation represented a giant and lasting step from naval designs and strategies that were centuries old.

Explosive devices not shot from small arms or artillery were a source of prewar interest. Crude kinds of hand grenades had been developed and had seen limited, restricted use. At Fort Sumter, Federal engineers filled huge barrels with gunpowder and planned to detonate them by using trails of powder.

Ironclad warships such as the Monitor *(left) and the* Virginia *made wooden naval vessels obsolete overnight.* [U.S. ARMY MILITARY HISTORY INSTITUTE]

It was not until the war became national in scope that someone devoted full time to experiments with special kinds of explosives. Confederate Brig. Gen. Gabriel Rains perfected a percussion cap so sensitive that it exploded on touch, igniting the powder with which it was connected.

At Yorktown, Virginia, many of the Rains devices were buried in front of Confederate positions. When men in gray withdrew, enemy forces advanced over ground strewn with primitive land mines. Forward movement came to an abrupt halt when a buried charge blew up, often wounding or killing those persons nearest it.

Union authorities were loud in their denunciation of the "infernal devices" that the Confederates had begun to call torpedoes. Their use was branded as "a savage mode of warfare." Yet Federal soldiers and scientists were busy developing new and more sophisticated torpedoes.

Arranged to float beneath the surface of water and to explode on contact, these were the torpedoes that Rear Adm. David G. Farragut damned at Mobile Bay. By war's end, both sides were producing and using torpedoes that could be exploded electrically.

Both sides also succeeded in producing "clockwork bombs" whose explosion was predetermined prior to their placement.

Twentieth-century missiles and rockets of every variety, including those drawn to their targets by heat, are descendants of Rains's earliest torpedoes.

Pondering ways to accelerate communication between commanders on the battlefield, George W. Beardslee perfected a mobile telegraph unit. Albert J. Meyer, the chief signal officer of Union forces, was quick to adopt the new Beardslee system.

A typical unit, packed in a wooden box, was the heart of the Federal "flying telegraph train." Containing about five miles of insulated wire, this portable military telegraph was transported in two wagons. Beardslee's invention was so successful that by 1864 few Federal commanders used the time-honored courier rider. Instead, their communications consisted largely of telegrams.

The Southerners never came close to producing or using mobile telegraph systems that were competitive with those of the Federals. No one knows how much this factor contributed to the eventual collapse of the Confederacy, but the predecessor of portable two-way radios soon was in use by civilian field crews of many kinds.

Floating torpedoes surfaced on nearly every body of water that could float a warship. [HARPER'S WEEKLY]

New weapons galore came from the industrial North. Col. Hiram Berdan of the First U.S. Sharpshooters was responsible for at least a half-dozen innovations. One of them, a long-distance range-finder, had a permanent effect upon the use of artillery throughout the world.

A Confederate officer devised a hand-cranked rapid-fire gun that could fire as many as sixty-five 1.57-inch shells per minute. Pro-duction facilities were so limited that this primitive machine gun is believed to have seen service only at the battle of Seven Pines.

Meanwhile, North Carolina native Richard J. Gatling perfected a gun designed to fire 250 rounds per minute. A few of them were used aboard Union warships and during the siege of Petersburg, but they had no significant impact upon the war. After the war, the physician who developed the first modern machine gun touted it as having been created to kill so rapidly that wars would cease to be waged.

Other less visibly dramatic changes than weapons development were taking place, and they had more profound long-range effects. For generations, it had been taken for granted that military nurses would be male members of fighting forces. This was about to change—forever.

Dorothea Dix arrived at the White House with a plan and a mis-sion. Presidential secretaries John G. Nicolay and John Hay recorded their satisfaction at "the arrival of Miss Dix, who comes to offer herself and an army of nurses to the government gratu-itously for hospital service." On June 10, 1861, she received a parchment unlike any ever before issued; for the first time the nation had a superintendent of U.S. Army nurses who was female.

Most veterans of military medicine reacted indignantly to Mother Dix's appointment. There were no general hospitals, but some of the larger installations had post hospitals. At Leavenworth, Kansas, there were accommodations for only twenty men.

Even after twenty-four members of the medical corps resigned to join the Confederacy, the U.S. Army still boasted a complement of twenty-seven surgeons and sixty-two assistant surgeons. With mili-tia units due to serve only ninety days, many could not understand what had influenced U.S. Secretary of War Simon Cameron to establish a corps of female nurses.

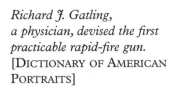

Richard J. Gatling,
a physician, devised the first
practicable rapid-fire gun.
[DICTIONARY OF AMERICAN
PORTRAITS]

That question became moot as the first Federal casualties reached Washington from the Manassas battlefield. Before the terrible carnage of the war ended, changing attitudes guaranteed that women would be welcomed to the nursing vocation.

Shortages of manpower opened other doors for women. A few bold spirits with good penmanship won early appointments as clerks in the U.S. Treasury Department. Soon women began to appear in the Patent Office and even in the U.S. War Department.

By early 1865, tens of thousands of women were government employees. Large corporations were beginning, grudgingly, to open their doors to a few women considered to be exceptionally capable. More than all other factors combined, the Civil War served as the foundation upon which the modern women's movement was erected.

A concurrent shift was also occurring at the highest levels of government. Founded from thirteen British colonies, the United States was for decades simply what the name implied: a union, or federation, of semiautonomous states.

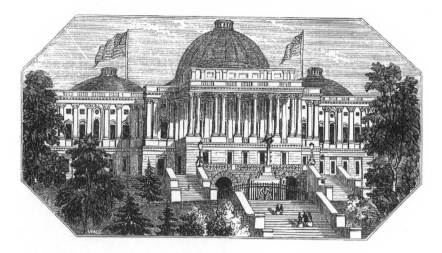

Prior to the war, the unfinished U.S. Capitol building symbolized the general weakness of the federal government. [GLEASON'S PICTORIAL, 1854]

Very early, it was clear to Lincoln and his colleagues that a loose conglomeration of political entities could not wage a successful war. Exerting what came to be called "war powers," the president took drastic actions that had the sanction of neither Congress nor the Constitution.

As the war progressed, the power concentrated in the Federal government expanded steadily. At the same time, rights and powers formerly relegated to the states were defined and limited. By the time Lincoln launched his campaign for a second term in the White House, the nature of the Union had been altered radically. With the central government now dominant, governors and legislators found themselves increasingly controlled from Washington.

This radical revision of the U.S. political structure soon began to advance with an impetus of its own. Federal programs, agencies, and regulations proliferated. Federal power loomed larger and larger in the everyday lives of ordinary citizens. In a real sense, the United States of the late twentieth century is the product of a radical shift in the bases of power that were initiated because they were essential to winning the war. If the debate of the early 1990s on downsizing the federal government succeeds, subsequent changes could revert the federal-state relationship to its pre–Civil War state.

CHAPTER

6

The Names Were Changed

Were the Civil War record to include only the birth names of fighting men, the account might be hard to recognize. At least three dozen familiar names differ from those of the originals. Many alterations were deliberately made, often for understandable reasons. Most came about informally and were never made legal. Others were by-products of events over which the owners of the names had no control.

Regardless of why they were fashioned, the altered names rather than the originals appear in the record. An estimated three hundred women joined the fighting forces in disguise; only a fraction of their real and assumed names are known with certainty. In other cases, an informally modified name was treated as though it were legal.

When their first child was born at Point Pleasant, Ohio, in 1822, Jesse R. Grant and his wife, the former Hannah Simpson, had a ready-made name for him. Hiram Ulysses grew up not realizing that part of his name came from classical mythology. He was keenly aware, though, that his schoolmates jeered at it. After all, very few youngsters are saddled with names whose initials form a word so potent among juveniles as "HUG." To reduce the teasing, the young Grant transposed his names and became Ulysses Hiram.

At age seventeen he set his sights on the U.S. Military Academy and persuaded everyone he knew to write to Rep. Thomas L. Hamer in his behalf. Hamer, who was not personally acquainted with Grant, duly appointed him to West Point. Hastily preparing the necessary papers, the lawmaker inadvertently used the maiden name of Grant's mother on the submission to the academy's admissions office.

When Grant presented himself for enrollment at the Point, he was surprised to find that he had been enrolled as Ulysses Simpson Grant. Since the change was acceptable to him, he made no protest. Once the modified name was entered in the official military record, it was never again changed.

From that clerical mistake came U. S. Grant—an almost providentially bestowed coincidence, both with the initials of his country and with an early high moment for Union forces in the West when Grant offered no terms for surrender to the Confederates at Fort Donelson, Tennessee. "Unconditional Surrender" Grant drew headlines from that moment, through two terms in the White House, and into history.

Hugh Judson Kilpatrick of New Jersey attended West Point fourteen years after Grant. Never having liked his first, baptismal name, which he considered effeminate, he casually introduced himself as Judson when his enrollment was being processed.

Busy with stacks of paperwork, the admissions clerks didn't bother to check the document attesting to the appointment of a farmer's son from Deckertown. With that annoying first name out of the way, Judson Kilpatrick graduated on May 6, 1861, and pinned on the insignia of a second lieutenant of artillery. Three days later he accepted a promotion to the rank of captain and was transferred from the U.S. Army to the Fifth New York Infantry.

In September, Kilpatrick was transferred again, this time to the Second New York Cavalry, and received another promotion. As a brigadier general, he led mounted men in every important action within the eastern theater of the war. Once having feared that he'd be called a sissy, Kilpatrick drove his men and horses so furiously that he came to be known as "Kill Cavalry."

Cadet Arnold Jones became uncomfortable with his surname some time before his 1837 graduation from West Point. Substituting the name of his paternal grandmother for that of his father, he became Arnold Elzey. Immediately after Fort Sumter he changed uniforms, becoming a Confederate lieutenant colonel. Just one year later he was Brigadier General Elzey.

Still another West Point cadet underwent a change of name at the academy. Born in Gates County, North Carolina, Laurence Simmons Baker received a congressional appointment in 1847. Re-

Hugh Judson Kilpatrick's first name was ignored by a careless clerk at West Point, and Kilpatrick never missed it. [HARPER'S WEEKLY]

porting for his first day of classes, when the roll was called, he discovered that a War Department clerk had altered his name to the more familiar spelling of Lawrence.

Service on the frontier in the U.S. Mounted Rifles ended when he switched uniforms. As colonel of the First North Carolina Cavalry, the Confederate officer led his men so effectively that he became a brigadier in just over a year.

Some future officers who never attended military academies became new persons figuratively when they enlisted for war service. Julian Scott of Vermont, a musician only fifteen years old, watched helplessly as he was given a middle initial by a clerk.

Carried on muster rolls as Julian A. Scott, the drummer boy became a stretcher bearer when men of his regiment were wounded. At age sixteen he received the Congressional Medal of Honor for gallantry under enemy fire.

John A. Drummond of Galveston, Texas, volunteered for Confederate service when he was about the same age as Scott. Fearing that his father would learn what he had done and would have him discharged as being underage, he enlisted as John Anderson. His father didn't discover the subterfuge until too late, so Anderson fought through much of the war as a member of the Davis Guards.

Frederick Henry Dyer was also under the legal age to enlist. Calling himself Frederick H. Metzger, in September 1863 he gained a berth as a musician in Company H of the Seventh Connecticut Infantry.

Dyer's unit fought at Olustee, Drewry's Bluff, the Bermuda Hundred, Chaffin's Farm, New Market Heights, Fort Fisher, and numerous other places. Mustered out on July 20, 1865, he settled in Philadelphia and built up a printing business.

Success in business wasn't enough for the veteran who changed his name in order to enlist as a boy. Aware that there was no reliable source of information about all Federal units, he decided to compile one. During five years in which he lived as a hermit, Dyer put together by hand a colossal *Compendium of the War of the Rebellion* that remains the standard work of its kind after more than eight decades.

Half a dozen or more fighting men modified their names into forms that made them seem to be descended from ancestors who lived in the British Isles.

Julius Szamvald became a lieutenant in the Austrian army, then joined a revolutionary movement that was crushed. As a refugee he spent time in both England and Germany before coming to the United States as journalist Julius Stahel. An organizer of the First German Rifles, he became a brigadier general of U.S. Volunteers on November 12, 1861.

Henry Beeger emigrated from Germany before the war. Calling himself Henry Bertran, he joined the U.S. Army because of the high pay scale it offered. After five years as a member of the Second Artillery, he tired of monotonous life in tiny camps and deserted. At the outbreak of conflict, the man from Germany became a first lieutenant in the First Wisconsin Infantry. Promoted grade-by-grade until he became a colonel, he was the only deserter to become a brevet brigadier as a reward for his services during the Civil War.

Unlike Beeger, George Pforr didn't settle for half-measures when he decided to anglicize his name. Calling himself Charles W. Anderson, he joined Company K of the First New York Cavalry.

Anderson didn't volunteer until February 1864, but he won a Congressional Medal of Honor a year later. At war's end he signed up for a hitch in Company M of the Third U.S. Cavalry and remained in uniform for a dozen more years. Discharged in April 1878, he settled in Staunton, Virginia, where his wife, his children, and his neighbors knew him only as George Pforr.

Determined to serve in the Eighth Texas Cavalry, Charles Pelham Ten Eyck was sure that his name would lead to hazing. Presenting himself as Charles T. Pelham, he fought with distinction until he was fatally wounded by a Federal ball.

His grieving parents successfully petitioned the Texas legislature to change the name of their only grandson. As a result, Charles Pelham Ten Eyck Jr. became known as Charles T. Pelham.

Born in the Ohio River town of Wheeling, then still a part of Virginia, Jesse Lee Renault desperately wanted to attend West Point. Fearful that a foreign-sounding surname associated with a sly fox would be an impediment, he began calling himself Jesse Reno.

Jesse graduated eighth in his class from the Point, a class that included Thomas J. Jackson, George Pickett, and George B. McClellan. These three fellow cadets compiled military records more impressive than that of the boy from Wheeling. After fifteen years in the U.S. Army, he became a brigadier general of U.S. Volunteers.

Yet the man who was mortally wounded at Fox's Gap, Virginia, on September 14, 1862, has a special monument of sorts. Alone among members of the West Point class of 1846, his name appears on the map of the United States. Had he not deliberately changed his name, today's Reno, Nevada, might have been Renault.

Ivan Vasilovich Turchinoff became a professional soldier in his native Russia and rose to the rank of colonel in the Imperial Guard. Upon settling in Chicago in 1856 he decided to do something about his name. As John Basil Turchin he soon found work in the engineering department of a railroad successfully sued by attorney Abraham Lincoln of Springfield.

Following the outbreak of war, Turchin left the Illinois Central Railroad to become colonel of the Nineteenth Illinois Infantry. Perhaps because his wife made a personal appeal to Lincoln, the man whose subordinates called him "the Russian Thunderbolt" received a commission as a brigadier general.

Ferdinand Heinrich Gustav Hilgard left his native Bavaria in 1853. Hoping to become a journalist, he changed his name to Henry Villard and became a Washington correspondent for a number of major newspapers. By 1863 he was a valued member of the staff of Horace Greeley, whose *New York Herald* was perhaps the most widely circulated paper in the nation.

Edward W. Hincks of Boston won a seat in the state legislature while quite young. Just ten days after Fort Sumter he decided to volunteer for military service but wanted to be regarded as a "genuine American."

With a single letter dropped from his name, Edward Hinks launched his military career as a second lieutenant in the famous Second Cavalry, U.S. Army. Less than eighteen months later, the man who considered his legal name to sound "distinctly foreign" was a brigadier general of U.S. Volunteers.

At least one professional soldier altered his name so that he would seem to have a pronounced foreign ancestry. Washington Carroll Tevis of Pennsylvania graduated from the U.S. Military Academy in 1849. Within a year he sensed opportunity abroad, so he changed his name to Nessim Bey and became a *bim-bachi* (major) in the Turkish army.

The outbreak of the Civil War induced him to return home and volunteer for service as C. Carroll Tevis. As a lieutenant colonel of Delaware and Maryland units, he compiled a long combat record. Congress accordingly made him a brevet brigadier general.

Other relatives made decisions that affected the lives of at least four youngsters. At the request of an uncle, Alexander Slidell, an officer of the U.S. Navy, added the name Mackenzie to his surname. His son was named Ranald Slidell Mackenzie. Immediately upon graduating from West Point in 1862, Ranald became an assistant engineer in the Ninth Corps. By 1864 he had been promoted to the rank of brigadier general of U.S. Volunteers, later becoming both a U.S. Army brevet brigadier and a brevet major general.

A youthful Cherokee, Galagina, studied in Connecticut at a school that received financial aid from Revolutionary War officer Elias

Boudinot. With the permission of the veteran of Washington's army, Galagina changed his name to that of his patron.

When a son was born to him in 1835, the boy did not take a tribal name but was known as Elias Cornelius Boudinot. He was secretary of the Arkansas convention that voted for secession. After having served as a representative of the Cherokee Nation, the man whose name sounded like that of a colonial of European background became a lieutenant colonel in a Confederate regiment of Cherokees.

Spanish-born George Ferrugut changed his name to Farragut when he fought in the American Revolution. While stationed at New Orleans, he became closely associated with Cmdr. David Porter.

Porter later took youthful James G. Farragut into his home and reared him as a foster son. In gratitude, the man whose surname had been changed by his father voluntarily altered his baptismal name to honor Porter. As a result, David G. Farragut took to the sea and became the first U.S. naval officer to be awarded the rank of full admiral.

Attorney Charles R. Sherman of Ohio considered the Native American warrior Tecumseh to be one of the greatest men of the region. He named his son in honor of the Shawnee chieftain. Relatives found the boy's name cumbersome, so they abbreviated it to Cump.

When Cump was nine years old, his father died suddenly, leaving his widow and eleven children all but destitute. Relatives and friends took the children into their homes and reared them as though they were their own.

Cump was adopted informally by wealthy Thomas Ewing, a neighbor. Soon Ewing insisted that the boy be baptized formally, decreeing that Cump must have "a proper Christian name." Since the day chosen was the feast day of Saint William, at Ewing's orders the priest christened the boy William Tecumseh.

The boy went on to be one of the most effective Union generals of the Civil War. Although he customarily signed all military documents as W. T. Sherman, among relatives and intimates he continued to be known as Cump or Cumpy.

Not all who changed their names or had them changed were male. At least four women gained fame or notoriety under names of their own choosing. Clarissa Harlow Barton of Oxford, Massachusetts,

The man who planned and led the March to the Sea was the namesake of the early nineteenth-century Shawnee leader Tecumseh. [AUTHOR'S COLLECTION]

tolerated her name while she was a schoolgirl. When she went to Washington to apply for a position in the U.S. Patent Office, however, she listed herself simply as Clara. Once selected, the shortened version of her name remained with her for the rest of her life. As a result, many a person who reveres the founder of the American Red Cross is not aware that, properly speaking, she should be remembered as Clarissa Barton.

A daughter born to slaves of Dorchester County, Maryland, worked as a maid, a field hand, a cook, and a woodcutter. Most other slaves on the plantation knew her simply as Aramenta, daughter of Harriet Greene.

Long before she became the wife of John Tubman, a free black, she had taken her mother's name and was known as Harriet. A leader in the Underground Railroad, Harriet Tubman helped an estimated three hundred slaves to freedom and is renowned as "the Moses of her people."

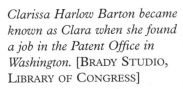

Clarissa Harlow Barton became known as Clara when she found a job in the Patent Office in Washington. [BRADY STUDIO, LIBRARY OF CONGRESS]

Largely forgotten today, Cincinnati native Delia Swift changed her name when she moved to New Orleans at about age thirteen. As a prostitute, pickpocket, and skilled mugger, Bridget Fury was well known locally.

Imprisoned in 1858 for murder, she was still behind bars when the city fell into Union hands. One of the first decrees from the new military governor, George F. Shepley, was a blanket pardon of all persons convicted prior to the Federal occupation. Elevated to the level of a folk heroine because of a self-chosen name that was strangely fitting, Bridget Fury was briefly notorious throughout much of the nation.

Ethelinda Eliot of Goshen, New York, was a descendant of John Eliot, known as "the apostle to the Indians." As an adolescent she began contributing poetry to newspapers and magazines.

Since she regarded her surname as "tame and commonplace," she customarily signed her lines as Ethel Lynn. At age nineteen, after becoming the bride of William H. Beers, her pen name became Ethel Lynn Beers.

After her 1849 escape from slavery, Harriet Tubman led scores of others to freedom. [NATIONAL ARCHIVES]

One of her many Civil War poems first appeared as "The Picket Guard" in the November 30, 1861, issue of *Harper's Magazine.* Remembered for its vivid first line, "All quiet along the Potomac tonight," the poem is seldom recognized as the product of a woman who chose for herself an elegant-sounding name. Instead, "All Quiet Along the Potomac" is usually thought to be the work of a veteran in blue who spent many nights on picket duty.

When a recruitment officer came to an Ohio town, a boy of ten decided he wanted to join the fight. His chances of being accepted as a drummer would be enhanced, he believed, if he had an important-sounding name. So John Clem hastily fabricated a middle name—Lincoln.

In April 1862 the nation came to know him as Johnny Shiloh. He seems to have been a drummer for several units before being added to the muster roll of Company C of the Twenty-second Michigan Infantry. At the battle of Chickamauga he won national fame, but that was not enough to gain admission to West Point at war's end. Brushed aside as having an inadequate education, the man who named himself for the president of the United States remained in uniform until his 1916 resignation as a major general.

Elihu Washburn of Maine began thinking about a career in politics before he was twenty years old. To make his name "properly elegant," he added an *e* to the end. Three of his brothers refused to follow his example. Although each of the trio of Washburns achieved national prominence during the war years, it was Elihu Washburne who was U.S. secretary of state before becoming the U.S. minister to France.

Born at Saint Augustine, Florida, young Edmund Kirby Smith fought through the Mexican War after graduating from West Point. He changed uniforms in 1861 and became a Confederate colonel of cavalry. Successively in command of a number of Confederate departments, he decided that Smith was too common a name to demand the respect he deserved.

Long predating the modern trend toward hyphenating names, he began calling himself Edmund Kirby-Smith. Although never made legal formally, it is his self-chosen modified name that appears in many reference works today.

Morgan Lewis Smith of New York was at least as contemptuous of his surname as was Kirby-Smith. Enlisting in the U.S. Army as Martin L. Sanford, he became a drill instructor. Five years' experience in that capacity made it easy for him to raise the Eighth Maine Infantry in 1861.

Correctly anticipating that his men would elect him to serve as their colonel, he resumed his legal name. The name of Martin L. Sanford appears nowhere in the lists of Civil War officers, but Morgan L. Smith became a brigadier general of U.S. Volunteers about one year after Fort Sumter.

Harriet Bailey, a slave on a Maryland plantation, became pregnant by a white man whose identity was not known. When her son was born, she decided to give him a truly sonorous name: Frederick Augustus Washington Bailey.

Years later, after having purchased his freedom, Harriet's son decided to sever his ties with the past. At the suggestion of a friend, he borrowed a surname from Sir Walter Scott's *Lady of the Lake*. A skilled orator and publicist, the man now known as Frederick Douglass was the only African American of his era to become an adviser to U.S. presidents.

Without having reasons so compelling as those that persuaded Frederick Bailey to change his name, Robert B. Smith of Virginia took similar action. Moving to Florida, he joined the staff of the *Tallahassee Floridian* as Robert Benjamin Hilton.

Hilton—or Smith—advanced professionally in journalism while also studying law. As owner and editor of the *Savannah Georgian,* he returned to Florida to become captain of the First Florida Infantry. Earlier having been elected to Congress, but never having been seated, he now won a seat in the Confederate Congress. After hostilities ceased, the lawmaker with an assumed name launched a new career as a judge.

Few U.S. lawmakers of the period were so influential as Sen. Henry Wilson. Having succeeded to the seat of nationally famous Edward Everett, Wilson was involved in many Washington intrigues. He was among the prominent men believed to have been lovers of Confederate spy Rose Greenhow O'Neal; earlier he had helped Clara Barton to gain her position in the patent office as a pioneer female employee of the U.S. government.

An ardent admirer and a staunch friend of Lincoln, Wilson engineered passage of an all-important congressional measure that granted Lincoln after-the-fact sanction of numerous irregular actions. Many lawmakers were wary of approving the measure, so the vote on the bill was stalled repeatedly.

With the special session about to end, a bill was introduced to boost the salaries of U.S. soldiers. In the aftermath of Bull Run, no senator or member of the House of Representatives would have dared vote against this measure. Wilson craftily attached a last-minute rider to the bill that conferred extraordinary war powers upon the first Republican president.

Long after he had shown himself to be a master of political maneuvering, Massachusetts voters discovered that their senator had been born in New Hampshire as Jeremiah Jones Colbaith. He had changed his name when he moved to the Bay State in 1833 and began work as a shoemaker.

An aristocratic Creole from Louisiana may have changed his name more often than any other notable of the Civil War. Born as Pierre Gustave Toutant-Beauregard, he deleted the hyphen while he was still quite young. Later he stopped using Pierre to become plain G. T. Beauregard.

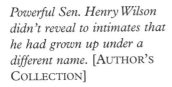

Powerful Sen. Henry Wilson didn't reveal to intimates that he had grown up under a different name. [AUTHOR'S COLLECTION]

By the time he had begun to win fame as a Confederate general, the man from Louisiana had restored the first segment of his baptismal name. Widely known as P. G. T. Beauregard, he insisted that his friends simply call him Peter.

Beauregard was famous in the South as the hero of both Fort Sumter and Manassas, but his name was never so widely familiar as was that of a native of England. When Henry Carter came to New York in 1848, he changed his name legally to Frank Leslie for reasons he never revealed,.

Frank Leslie's Illustrated Newspaper competed with the famous *Harper's Weekly* to portray the war on paper. Because of its tremendous impact—still significant after many decades—his newspaper and its woodcuts and engravings made the name of Frank Leslie widely familiar.

Also a native of the British Isles, John Rowlands was a cabin boy on a merchant vessel. When it reached New Orleans shortly before the outbreak of the Civil War, Rowlands jumped ship. A wealthy merchant, Henry Morton Stanley, adopted the eighteen-year-old in 1859.

As a gesture of gratitude to his benefactor, the runaway changed his name and also became known as Henry Morton Stanley.

Stanley's Civil War career—one of the most varied and colorful on record—turned him toward the field of journalism. Eight years after shedding his uniform, he received a prized commission. James Gordon Bennett of the *New York Herald* put him in charge of an expedition to find an English doctor believed to be lost in central Africa. It was there that the journalist offered a greeting that was soon familiar throughout the Western world: "Dr. Livingstone, I presume?"

CHAPTER
7

Their Mothers Wouldn't Have Known Them

Joseph Howard of the *New York Times* was in or near Willard's Hotel in Washington, D.C., very early in the morning of February 23, 1861, when Abraham Lincoln arrived from Springfield. A telegram informed his editors that the president-elect had reached the capital wearing "a Scotch plaid cap and a very long military cloak, so that he was entirely unrecognizable."

Howard's headline-producing account was based on the fact that warnings of assassination had reached Lincoln in Philadelphia. As a result, a last-minute change of schedule sent him through Baltimore at an hour when no one was expecting him.

There had been no attempt at disguise, however. A soft wool hat given to Lincoln in New York was worn instead of his customary tall, stiff hat. Still, the peculiar hour and the story in the *Times* triggered hundreds of newspaper accounts. Numerous cartoons published before the first shot of the war was fired alleged that Lincoln had reached Washington so carefully disguised that no one who saw him would recognize him.

Strangely, another story of a chief executive in disguise surfaced around the time the last shots of the war were being fired. Northern newspapers reported that Jefferson Davis had been dressed as a woman at the time of his capture in Georgia. On May 27, *Harper's Weekly* depicted Davis in a long dress and surrounded by Federal soldiers. Like the Lincoln story and the ensuing cartoons, this scene was a fabrication, too. When Davis was apprehended on May 10, he had been dressed for riding and had thrown a raincoat over his shoulders.

Clement Vallandigham of Ohio, an influential Democrat and a pacifist, was arrested in the middle of the night. [HARPER'S WEEKLY]

Clement L. Vallandigham of Ohio was probably the most notable political figure who tried to disguise himself. Having been banished to Confederate territory, the one-time pacifist editor found himself unwelcome and unwanted. So the articulate advocate for peace went to Canada.

Ohio Democrats were outraged at the treatment of their former congressman. At a state convention, they nominated him for governor by a vote of 411 to 11. Partly because Lincoln actively worked for his opponent, Vallandigham lost the election by one hundred thousand votes in the October 1863 election.

Weary of exile, Vallandigham decided to return to Ohio in June 1864. For this momentous journey, the man whose face was familiar throughout the North stuffed a pillow under his clothing and tied on a set of false whiskers. When an account of his disguise became public, Lincoln mocked Vallandigham's attempt to conceal his identity.

Although he succeeded in ignoring arrest orders and reached Ohio, Vallandigham never again played a notable role in national politics. Edward Everett Hale used him as the model for the central character of his short story "The Man Without a Country."

Throughout the war, men and women of the North and of the South played ludicrous or thrilling roles in disguise. In Saint Louis, Capt. Nathaniel Lyon wanted a firsthand look at a nearby Southern military camp. On May 9, 1861, the veteran U.S. Army officer turned into "old Mrs. Alexander, a society matron who liked to wear bombazine and a heavy black veil." Sometimes described as having disguised himself as a farm woman, Lyon did pose as a woman of wealth. He probably borrowed the clothes from the mother-in-law of Rep. Francis P. Blair Jr.

Regardless of where he secured his elaborate dress and bonnet, the disguised Lyon climbed into a carriage with a black driver. Since the real Mrs. Alexander was well known for her eccentricities, the officer made a leisurely tour of Camp Jackson without incident.

According to the *Memphis Appeal*, a Confederate scouting party led by a Colonel Looney left Chattanooga in late November 1861. "They captured fourteen horses, and took one hundred Lincoln men prisoners," the newspaper reported. A Unionist ruffian known only as Holloway "managed to make his escape by clothing himself in female attire."

In divided Kentucky, guerrilla bands flourished. One of them was led by prosperous but tiny Marcellus J. Clarke. According to the *Louisville Courier*, he was frequently disguised as Sue Mundy and continued a double life until March 15, 1865. As he swung from a gallows after a hasty "citizens' trial," there was no doubt that the guerrilla leader was male.

Recent studies indicate that tales about Sue Mundy's exploits were greatly exaggerated by reporters for the *Louisville Daily Journal*. Even if that is the case, few men were as successful as Clarke had been in maintaining a long-time pretense at being an attractive woman.

Capt. Frank H. Mason of the Twelfth Ohio Volunteer Cavalry was a member of the force that captured men who had fought under Confederate Maj. Gen. Joseph Wheeler. Near Atlanta, following

Johnston's surrender in North Carolina, Wheeler and his raiders were surrounded and trapped.

Because a captured slave in the group wore the uniform of a Confederate major general, a Federal officer became suspicious. Soon he discovered that Wheeler had exchanged clothing with his valet in a futile attempt to be identified as a contraband, or a rootless slave. After his disguise had been exposed, Wheeler was sent to Fort Warren as a prisoner of war.

Only a handful of men are known to have disguised themselves as former slaves. One band, whose names were not preserved, successfully made it out of a temporary prison in Saint Louis by using burnt cork on their hands and faces.

Brig. Gen. Schuyler Hamilton, commander of the Federal military district in which the escape occurred, took quick steps to prevent more Confederates from using the same ruse. He directed that the prison's doctor examine all inmates and "to exclude from the prison all negroes," for whom a temporary shelter was arranged elsewhere.

Col. Richard Thomas of the Virginia Volunteers fared better than did the Confederate cavalry leader who tried to pose as a runaway slave. His caper in disguise began in June 1862, when a plan was made to seize the USS *Pawnee*. The warship's armament made conventional capture impossible. Thomas therefore decided to seize a small steamer, the *St. Nicholas,* with the hope that he might approach his target without raising an alarm.

Capt. George N. Hollins of the Confederate navy, dressed as a woman companion, went along as chief aide to Thomas. Other volunteers were dressed as workmen. Concealing their weapons in tool boxes, these "laboring men" went aboard the *St. Nicholas* at three or four different points.

When the little steamer reached Point Lookout, Maryland, a woman in a hoop skirt came aboard and registered herself as "a French lady named Zarvona." Officers of the little steamer were honored to have aboard so exotic a passenger and expressed disappointment when she said she must go to her cabin and rest.

Soon after "Zarvona" went below, a Confederate Zouave wearing a brace of pistols climbed on deck. His men pulled out their weapons and took over the ship with little or no resistance. Learning that the *Pawnee* was not at her customary berth, the seized vessel was taken up the Rappahannock River toward Fredericksburg and transformed into the CSS *Rappahannock.*

Leading only four men from the *Rappahannock,* "Zarvona" soon boarded a larger passenger steamer where "she" was quickly recognized. By the time a company of Federal infantry had swarmed aboard, the French "lady" had seemed to vanish. After a ninety-minute search, however, "she" was found curled up in a bureau drawer. Once flushed from hiding, the "lady" was revealed to be Thomas. So much publicity followed this incident that the man who had posed as a woman was for a time the most celebrated prisoner in Federal captivity.

At least one man who served a brief term as an irregular soldier did not gain any fame until after the fighting had ceased. Small of stature and having little or no beard, smooth-skinned young Jesse James sometimes disguised himself as a woman to scout Federal positions.

Pvt. Benjamin F. Stringfellow of the Fourth Virginia Cavalry had light-colored hair and weighed less than a hundred pounds. To Capt. John F. Lay that seemed to make him an ideal candidate for the risky job of spying.

Properly dressed, he was described by admiring comrades as "making a really attractive girl." Mincing slightly as he walked, Stringfellow went into Federal-occupied Arlington, Virginia, several times. The information he gathered is said to have proved especially useful to Confederate Gen. P. G. T. Beauregard.

Confederates who made the northernmost raid of the war knew that they were risking their lives. Preparing to rob the banks of Saint Albans, Vermont, Pvt. William Teavis decided to don women's clothing. Some of his comrades jeered at his lack of courage, but Teavis was the only raider to get through the North without being detected.

For Secret Service agents and spies, disguise seemed to come naturally. Allan Pinkerton, who worked for Maj. Gen. George B. McClellan, claimed frequently to have spent days behind Confederate lines with his face and clothing so altered that even his mother would not have recognized him. His firsthand account is not supported by independent sources. He gave no hint of the way that a man from Chicago could disguise his voice and visit Memphis without detection.

Confederate spy Thomas N. Conrad had a voice so booming that it was useless to attempt to alter it when he penetrated Federal lines. His most conspicuous facial features were a huge mustache and a beard, carefully described to Federal commanders with whom he was likely to come into contact.

Conrad somehow turned what seemed a liability into an asset. He managed to alter his facial hair so that when in disguise he was not recognized by friends who had known him for years.

According to the *Louisville Journal* of November 30, 1861, an unidentified Confederate colonel was arrested at Paducah, Kentucky, "Dressed like an ordinary farmer, in conversation he appeared not very bright." When he became excited, his use of language changed so drastically that a fellow traveler asked the provost marshal to take him into custody.

During heavy fighting in Missouri, Federal leaders had urgent reasons to send dispatches from Sedalia to Independence. Since the region was heavily pocketed with Confederates, it was decided to seek volunteers for the ninety-mile mission.

Two Hoosiers, Pvts. Marshall Storey and William Waters, offered to undertake the long and dangerous journey. With dispatches hidden in their hats and boots, they assumed the role of refugees.

Once they were ordered to halt by the leader of a band of jay-hawkers, guerrilla fighters with Unionist leanings who used the war for their own purposes. Waters whispered to Storey, "Go along with me!" Pretending to be half-witted, the Federal soldier stammered that he was taking his brother home after a stay in Saint Louis.

His self-chosen role as a half-wit proved so successful that Waters tried to climb aboard a beautiful black pony belonging to a jay-hawker. When pulled from the animal's back he picked up a stick and pretended to challenge the owner to a fight.

With the laughter of their would-be captors ringing in their ears, the two Hoosiers left the band of jayhawkers and reached Independence with their messages intact.

Lafayette C. Baker, here depicted in a general's uniform, regularly posed as a photographer during his intelligence-gathering missions. [HARPER'S HISTORY OF THE CIVIL WAR]

Confederate Capt. Julius de Lagnel tried a similar ploy. Separated from his unit during heavy fighting in West Virginia, he stumbled upon a cabin in the mountains.

During three days in his refuge, de Lagnel carefully studied the mannerisms and speech patterns of the mountain family. He then set out to rejoin his comrades. Frequently stopped by Union pickets and guards, his "mountain accent and crackerish ways" convinced them that he was a farmer hunting livestock that had wandered from his pasture.

One of Pinkerton's agents, Pryce Lewis, posed as an English gentleman traveling for pleasure. Wearing tweeds and flourishing a cigar case ornamented with an ivory British lion, he had no difficulty in deceiving Secessionists of western Virginia during June 1861.

Lafayette C. Baker of the National Detective Police made several forays into Confederate territory. He drove a photographer's wagon and carried along the increasingly familiar tools of the trade. According to his reports, the Confederates from whom he gathered information were too interested in what the photographer was doing to ask questions about his identity.

Little is known about John Burke, a man who tried to spy for both sides, except that he had a glass eye and that he gave himself the honorary title of captain. It was the missing eye that enabled him to alter his appearance radically. When he left his glass eye behind to go on a mission, even close acquaintances failed to recognize him.

Confederate scout Henry B. Shaw (sometimes known as Capt. C. E. Coleman) took on the name and attire of an itinerant doctor so he could go back and forth between lines in Middle Tennessee.

Near Chambersburg, Pennsylvania, Confederate Col. Ashby Turner posed as a "horse doctor," or veterinarian, to spy for Stonewall Jackson.

Disguised as civilians, Capt. W. F. Brown and ten members of the Confederate Marine Corps took passage on the steamer *Ike Davis*. Once away from Federal installations, they seized the vessel and took it to Matagorda Bay, Texas, as a prize of war.

Federal soldiers proved equally adept at playing the same game. Capt. Peter Haggerty disguised himself as an organ grinder to go into Baltimore daily to gather information for Maj. Gen. Benjamin F. Butler. During one of his forays he learned that several tons of gunpowder had been stored on Calhoun Street. This information helped convince Butler that he should establish martial law in the city that seemed to be filled with secessionists.

After the battle of Wilson's Creek, Brig. Gen. Franz Sigel dressed like a Texas Ranger. Wearing a blanket over his uniform and topped by a yellow slouch hat, he passed through Confederate outposts without being challenged.

Members of Ohio regiments who volunteered for special service under James J. Andrews were not so fortunate. Dressed as civilians, they seized the locomotive *General* and set out to disrupt the railroad linking Atlanta with Chattanooga. After a ninety-mile chase, Andrews's raiders were captured.

Southern sympathies were so blatant in Baltimore that Federal spies were sent to the city. [THE SOLDIER IN OUR CIVIL WAR]

Because they were not in uniform, seven Union soldiers who posed as Confederate civilians were sentenced to die. Their mass execution in Atlanta was the railroad center's largest such event ever.

Richard Yates, wartime governor of Illinois, launched his military career at Bull Run. Late in the conflict he attracted the attention of Maj. Gen. Philip Sheridan, who requested him to organize a body of "special scouts." Actually spies, the fifty-eight men who made up

During a ninety-mile chase, Andrews's raiders often stopped to tear up track and try to burn bridges. [AUTHOR'S COLLECTION]

Yates's band frequently risked the gallows by donning Confederate uniforms in pursuit of information or other behind-the-lines actions.

Confederate Maj. Gen. James Ewell Brown "Jeb" Stuart took the same risk near Falling Waters, Virginia (now West Virginia). Unwilling to trust the skill and judgment of his subordinates, he wore a Federal uniform to scout the countryside ahead of his force.

Confederate Brig. Gen. Robert S. Hoke was in desperate need of a way to stall Federal forces entrenched near Drewry's Bluff, just north of Richmond. Explaining that the risk of death was great, he asked for a volunteer to undertake a special mission.

Pvt. Halifax R. Wood, age eighteen, immediately stepped forward. Hoke handed him a Federal uniform and issued verbal instructions. Hoke gathered no information, but the disguised Confederate made his way to the headquarters of Maj. Gen. Benjamin F. Butler and excitedly reported having seen a large force of Confederates landing on the James River. Having delivered the false message, the Confederate beat a hasty retreat to the safety of his own lines.

Also near Richmond, French soldier of fortune Victor Vifquain devised an outlandish scheme to end the war. With three companions, he donned a heavy disguise and headed toward the Confederate capital. Although his identity was not discovered, he was turned back by pickets before he could carry out his mission: to capture Jefferson Davis, president of the Confederacy.

In Richmond, Davis personally approved a plan submitted to him by Congressman Duncan F. Kenner of Louisiana. Kenner would travel to Europe in disguise and discuss with various government officials the possibility of abolishing slavery in the Confederacy in return for diplomatic recognition.

Knowing that he would have to pass through New York to reach his objective, Kenner resorted to an elaborate disguise. He made his long journey safely and without being recognized—but accomplished nothing. Realizing that the fate of the Confederacy had been sealed on battlefields, the European leaders were no longer interested in the possibility of extending diplomatic recognition to the new nation.

A few months after the start of hostilities, a special agreement between the two opposing forces exempted military surgeons from capture. Capt. Harry White of a Pennsylvania regiment decided to take advantage of this special opportunity.

As a prisoner of war, at City Point, Virginia, White went aboard a Confederate steamer carrying a small black valise that held a few surgical instruments. He successfully passed himself off as exempt from imprisonment until the captain of the vessel found his name on a list of officers not eligible for exchange. "Harry White, come forth!" bellowed an officer in gray. Momentarily forgetting his disguise, the officer from the Keystone State stepped from the ranks and ruefully relinquished his little black bag.

Henry B. Shaw, a steamboat clerk intimately acquainted with Middle Tennessee, headed a band of spies who worked for Confederate Brig. Gen. Benjamin F. Cheatham. Disguised as a rural physician recently having accepted a gray uniform, he called himself Dr. C. E. Coleman.

Union forces didn't know that Coleman was an aide to Gen. Braxton Bragg, so they permitted the doctor to wander through their lines at will. Coleman and others who made up a special body of scouts always wore Confederate uniforms when on a mission. If captured, the uniform would allow them to be treated as prisoners of war rather than as spies.

Chaplin J. D. Rodgers of the Twenty-third Indiana Infantry may have heard of the caper pulled off in Missouri by fellow Hoosiers. Whether that was the case or not, he was immediately suspicious when an elderly gentleman boarded a vessel at Henderson, Kentucky.

Dressed like a farmer, the man started a conversation with Rodgers and acted dull-witted. In a moment of excitement, however, the rhythm and pitch of his voice made a decided change. At Paducah, therefore, Rodgers called the attention of the provost marshal to the man who was playing the role of a dullard.

Questioned, the old farmer turned out to be a Confederate colonel who had participated in the battle of Bull Run. He was immediately taken into custody, but his name and unit were not recorded.

Federal scout Henry H. Young and a band of more than fifty men made numerous successful forays into Confederate territory disguised as Southern soldiers.

Capt. Alexander M. Shannon and handpicked men of the Eighth Texas Cavalry pursued a similar course. Wearing blue uniforms, they gathered information on movements of Federal troops in Tennessee and Georgia.

All correspondents had been barred from the funeral service for Maj. Gen. Philip Kearny, killed by a Confederate bullet on September 1, 1862. Joseph Howard of the *New York Times* had earlier written a bogus account of Lincoln's pre-inaugural journey in disguise. This time, he donned a surplice and carried a prayer book to cover the ceremony and give readers a firsthand report of the funeral.

A few women proved to be at least as resourceful and skillful as the men who had disguised themselves. Several authorities agree that the Civil War saw enough women fighting in uniform to make up

Dressed as a man, Loreta Velaques briefly led a Confederate company at the first battle of Manassas. [COLORFUL WOMEN OF THE WAR, 1872]

several companies. Some of them seem never to have been discovered; others were identified under strange circumstances.

A Brooklyn girl known only as Emily dressed as a young boy and enlisted in a Michigan regiment as a drummer. After she was fatally wounded during the second day's fighting at Chickamauga, a male nurse attempting to bandage her wound discovered her secret.

Loreta Velaques of New Orleans dressed as Lt. Harry Buford so she could accompany her husband to war. Said to have served briefly as a company commander under Confederate Brig. Gen. Bernard Bee at Manassas, her comrades in arms learned her secret a year later. According to her colorful memoirs, she then became a secret agent.

Like Velaques, Florena Budwin posed as a man so she could go into battle with her husband. Both were captured and sent to the military prison at Andersonville, where he died. Florena somehow survived and was sent to another Confederate prison at Florence, South Carolina. When she was caught up in an epidemic of illness, the doctor who discovered her sex offered her a special room plus food not served to ordinary prisoners.

Albert J. Cashier of the Ninety-fifth Illinois Regiment fought at Vicksburg, Nashville, and Mobile. Fifty years after enlisting, Cashier was injured in an automobile accident. At a hospital, Cashier was discovered to be a female. Questioned, she admitted nothing except that she was of Irish birth and was really named Hodgers.

An even later discovery took place in 1934 near Shiloh National Military Park. Digging in his garden, Mancil Milligan found a quantity of human bones. He eventually learned that he had stumbled upon the unmarked grave of nine Federal soldiers killed in the battle.

While Milligan's find evoked wide interest in the region, it was not until pathologists examined them that a more interesting discovery was made. One set of bones belonged to a female, probably killed or fatally wounded by the minié ball that lay close to her ribs.

Investigation failed to identify the woman who died at Shiloh. According to some authorities, however, she was the only female positively known to have been killed in combat.

No other woman who posed as a man quite equaled the exploits of Sarah Edmonds. Calling herself Franklin Thompson, she enlisted in the Second Michigan Infantry on May 14, 1861. Having escaped injury at Antietam, she contracted malaria a few months later. Knowing that a medical examination would prove her undoing, she deserted and for a time worked as a spy.

According to her account, in this role she often wore "a wig of real Negro wool" to play the role of a male slave. So disguised, she claimed to have visited Richmond several times.

In 1884 Sarah attended a regimental reunion minus her disguise as Franklin Thompson. Former comrades persuaded her to petition Congress for revocation of her conviction as a deserter and to file for a veteran's pension. She seems to have won both contests, for some records of the Grand Army of the Republic suggest that Sarah Emma Edmonds was its sole female member.

At about the time Jefferson Davis was falsely accused of trying to hide his identity by dressing as a woman, several notable Confederate leaders were traveling in disguise. Judah P. Benjamin, whose last post in the Richmond government was that of secretary of state, headed for Mexico after the capital fell. Since he spoke excellent French, he passed himself off as a Frenchman named Bonfal. Successively posing at different times as a sea cook and an ordinary farmer, the disguised former cabinet official reached Florida and found passage to England.

Maj. Gen. Jubal A. "Jubilee" Early also believed that he could find a haven south of the border. Famous—or infamous—for his Washington raid of 1864, he knew that his face was widely known. Permitting his beard to become scruffy, he reached Mexico wearing overalls and a straw hat appropriate for the dirt farmer he pretended to be.

8

Naval Chaos

Many battles were known to Confederates by one name, to Federals by another. The nomenclature of armies was an additional source of confusion; for example, the Army of the Tennessee was made up of men wearing blue, while the Army of Tennessee was a Confederate force.

Difficult as it was and still is to keep straight the many names used on land for the same event or similar reference, these are easy when compared to naval affairs. There were no standard procedures with respect to a change of possession. Following purchase or capture, a vessel's name might be retained or it might be altered. Frequently modified in naval records, but not always changed in civilian mercantile annals, the names of ships were a source of frustration to the officers whose duty it was to get them right.

Purchased by Rear Adm. Hiram Paulding in 1862 for $25,000, the *Nuestra Senora de Regla* displaced 376 tons. Men who stumbled over the name of the side-wheel steamer were delighted when she was recommissioned as the USS *Commodore Hull*.

Numerous men were honored by Federal authorities when their names were given to newly completed vessels or those purchased after having been in operation for months or years.

At the New York prize court, $331 was paid in 1863 for the captured ship *Hettiwan*. When it was launched under the Stars and Stripes, it bore the name *Percy Drayton*. Drayton had commanded the *Pocahontas* at the 1861 battle of Port Royal, facing Confederate guns under the command of his brother, Confederate Brig. Gen. Thomas F. Drayton.

The USS De Kalb *honored a German mercenary who had fought in the American Revolution.* [PICTORIAL HISTORY OF THE AMERICAN REVOLUTION]

The War Department obligingly transferred to the U.S. Navy the steamer *Lancaster.* When it became a member of the famous Ellett Marine Brigade, officials turned to a Revolutionary hero from abroad and called it the *Kosciuszko.*

The citizens of the great river city seemed not to have protested when the *Saint Louis* was renamed to honor another European Revolutionary War hero, the *Baron De Kalb.* As a tribute to the Marquis de Lafayette, the name of the *Fort Henry* was scrapped in favor of his. Earlier, the vessel had been registered as the *Alick Scott.*

Rated at 512 tons, the *Ethan Allen* commemorated still another hero of the American Revolution. When put to use fighting Confederates, it became the USS *Commodore Barney.*

Nearly twice as large, the *Atlantic* was purchased at New York in August 1863. Once it became the property of the U.S. Navy, its name was changed to honor *Commodore Read.*

When captured by the USS *Pursuit,* the 460-ton *Florida* became a prize of war. Purchased for $28,500 at an auction, the one-time Confederate ship became the USS *Hendrick Hudson.*

The blockade-runner Savannah *brought only $1,250 when sold at auction.* [PICTORIAL HISTORY OF THE CONFEDERACY]

Annals of the period say little about Ben Williams. Still, he must have been pleased when his name was bestowed upon a sailing vessel familiar on many waterfronts as the *Mediator.*

One of the most unusual changes involving a noteworthy person was made at Key West. There the Navy Department secured from the prize court the schooner *Priscilla C. Ferguson.* Despite the fact that a general by the same name had watched over the bombardment of Fort Sumter and had commanded Confederate forces at the first battle of Manassas, the 101-ton sailing vessel became the USS *Beauregard.*

Launched in 1819, a vessel called the *Alabama* was viewed askance once the state for which it was named withdrew from the Union. Yet it was not until 1864 that it belatedly became the USS *New Hampshire* in honor of one of the few states that was nearly 100 percent loyal.

Pocahontas, as conceived by an English artist, was commemorated by a Federal warship. [AUTHOR'S COLLECTION]

Early in the struggle, the schooner *Savannah*, a privateer out of Charleston, was captured. Condemned by a New York prize court, it was sold to the U.S. Navy for just $1,250. Armed with two 9-inch Dahlgren smoothbores and an 11-inch rifled cannon, the one-time Confederate vessel was added to the Potomac River Flotilla as the USS *Chotank*.

Another privateer proudly bore the name of the Confederate governor of North Carolina. Captured, the *A. D. Vance* soon became the *Winslow* and then the USS *Frolic*.

Indian names abounded among warships built for the U.S. Navy on contract. Only a few vessels captured or purchased were given new names from this source during the war years, however.

Purchased at Boston in 1855 for $55,000, the sailing sloop-of-war *City of Boston* was renamed *Despatch*. Five years later, with the attack on Fort Sumter a probability, the *Despatch* became the *Pocahontas* in honor of the Indian princess of Virginia's early colonial days.

Ulysses S. Grant used the *New Uncle Sam* in his expedition against Fort Donelson, Tennessee. Despite its role in that significant Federal victory, the 902-ton side-wheel steamer became the USS *Black Hawk* in December 1862.

Less than half the size of the vessel familiar to many as the *New Uncle Sam*, the screw steamer *Westernport* was big enough to hold four 32-pounder guns and one 24-pounder. Before the former mercantile vessel went to war, though, she became the USS *Wyandotte*.

Ironically, the retention of old names was often a source of as much confusion as would have resulted from changes. In an alphabetized sampling of major Union vessels, the first letter reveals these potential problems:

- Three vessels were called *Aries*.
- Half a dozen bore the name *Arizona*.
- *Arkansas* was honored by three ships and *Arletta* by two.
- Sailors served aboard five vessels called *Arrow* and two that were named *Artist*.
- The name *Ascension* was at the bows of three ships.
- Ten Federal vessels of widely varying size and strength were called the *Atlantic*.
- A figure of classical mythology gave his name to two ships called *Atlas* and three were called by the Latin-derived name of *Augusta*.
- *Aurora* was painted on four vessels, while there were two each of the *Avenger*, the *Avon*, and the *Azalea*.

Animals fared better than Native Americans when new names were bestowed upon Federal ships. The purchase of the wooden stern-wheel steamer *Rachel Miller* added significantly to the strength of the Mississippi River Flotilla. Soon after changing hands at Cincinnati, its feminine name was dropped in favor of the USS *Reindeer*.

A distant relative of the reindeer was commemorated when the 162-ton *Countess* was renamed the USS *Elk*.

Measuring 158 feet 8 inches in length, with a beam of more than 30 feet, the *Fanny Barker* became the USS *Fawn* as soon as she was equipped with six 24-pounder howitzers and entered Federal service.

Built at Cincinnati, the *Florence Miller No. 2* caught the eye of Adm. D. D. Porter, who paid $32,000 for her. When she became the property of the U.S. Navy, the riverboat entered her new career as the USS *Moose*.

The *Emma Brown* became the USS *Gazelle*, and the *Ohio Valley* was transformed into the USS *Ibex*.

Possibly the existence of a Confederate raider known as the *Alabama* led the new Federal owners of an 80-ton schooner named *Alabama* to rechristen it as the USS *Fox*.

Compared with the Federal records, those concerning Confederate ships are skimpy. Yet Richmond leaders were responsible for perhaps the most memorable of all changes of ships' names. When an attempt was made by the Federals to burn the USS *Merrimac* to prevent its capture, its name had already been shortened from the original *Merrimack*. Converted by its captors into the first American ironclad ready for battle, it became the famous CSS *Virginia*. Because a majority of early writers about the switch from wooden to iron vessels were from the North, the salvaged ship that bore the name of a Confederate state is still widely identified as having been the *Merrimac*.

Compared with many Federal vessels, the armament of the CSS *Savannah* was puny; she was mounted with only one 32-pounder smoothbore. Formerly the *Everglade*, this 53-ton warship created new confusion when she became the *Oconee* in August 1863.

Once called the *Leopard*, a privateer trying to outrun half a dozen blockaders failed to make it into Charleston Harbor. In desperation, its captain burned the splendid *Stonewall Jackson*, thereby failing to deliver 40,000 army shoes, 200 barrels of saltpeter, and several artillery pieces.

A sister vessel, the CSS *Stonewall*, went through the war relatively unscathed. She then ended her service in Japan as the *Hijms Allzuma*.

Alexander H. Stephens of Georgia, vice president of the Confederacy. [LIBRARY OF CONGRESS]

Launched as the *Dragon* and renamed the *Torpedo,* a sleek river vessel received a special honor in 1864. She was selected to convey Confederate Vice President Alexander H. Stephens to Hampton Roads to engage in conversations aimed at achieving what Confederates considered an honorable peace.

When captured by the raider *Alabama,* the bark *Conrad* was promptly put under the Stars and Bars as the privateer *Tuscaloosa.* Earlier, Confederate acquisition of the *Giraffe* led her to become the *Robert E. Lee.*

Built in Boston, the 387-ton *Enoch Train* was a fixture around the New Orleans waterfront. Purchased for $100,000, she was given a protective coat of iron but only one 32-pounder carronade when converted into the CSS *Manassas.* No match for a powerful Federal warship, she was sunk in a battle below New Orleans after just three months' service in the Confederate navy.

When Southerners became her owner, the *Oreto* was renamed the CSS *Florida.* After an epoch-making voyage as a blockade-runner loaded to the gunwales with weapons and military supplies, the renamed *Fingal* reached Savannah. Soon afterward she became the CSS *Atlanta.*

Confederate purchasing agent James Bulloch, who accompanied the *Fingal* on her first voyage, wangled the purchase of numerous fine British-built vessels. One of them, built simply as *#290*, became first the *Enrica* and then the *Alabama*, the most famous cruiser to prey on Union shipping.

Despite the impact of the *Alabama*, Bulloch's most famous purchase in England was the swift raider initially known as the *Sea King*. Equipped with both sails and a 250-horsepower engine, this teak-plated clipper was rated at only 1,018 tons.

Commanded by Lt. James I. Waddell and renamed in honor of a Virginia valley, the *Shenandoah* captured thirty-eight prizes before being surrendered at Liverpool in 1865. Later purchased by the sultan of Zanzibar, the one-time raider went down in the Indian Ocean in 1879 under a third name that was not preserved in Western records.

Seeking to resupply Maj. Robert Anderson and his men at Fort Sumter, President James Buchanan dispatched the *Star of the West* to Charleston in January 1861. She was turned back by fire from cadets at The Citadel military college but was present at several other engagements before being captured.

Joyful Confederates went through formal ceremonies renaming the vessel the CSS *Saint Philip*, then ruefully decided to sink her. She went down in Mississippi's Tallahatchie River as part of an effort to block its channel to Federal vessels.

Like the *Alabama*, the CSS *Theodora* sailed under two earlier names. When launched, the 500-ton sidewheel ironclad privateer was called the *Carolina*. Before becoming a member of the Confederate fleet she was for a time listed as the *Gordon*.

U.S. Secretary of the Navy Gideon Welles or one of his top aides must have had a penchant for blossoms. One after another, several names of vessels were changed in favor of flowers.

Purchased in 1862 from a veteran tar who had given his surname to his ship, the little 117-foot *Schultz* became the USS *Columbine* as soon as she was acquired by the U.S. Navy.

A voyage to Charleston by the Star of the West *brought about the first shots of the war.* [HARPER'S HISTORY OF THE CIVIL WAR]

Secured at New York in 1863, the screw steamer *Governor* would seem to have had a satisfactory name. Not so, said Washington. Hence the far from dainty 198-ton vessel was renamed the USS *Camelia*.

On August 24, 1863, the very day she was purchased from A. H. Cunningham, the 82-ton *Ajax* became the USS *Carnation*. Acquired a few weeks later from J. Howe and C. W. Copeland, their 123-foot *Meteor* was immediately dubbed the USS *Cowslip*.

Apparently the use of feminine names was not welcomed in some circles. Brand new and sheathed with yellow metal, the tugboat *Alice* of Philadelphia became the property of the U.S. Navy in July 1864. The ink on the ownership papers was hardly dry before the 122-foot screw steamer was renamed the USS *Aster*.

Mary Gandy seemed an appropriate name for a 321-ton screw steamer while she was operated by Copeland and Howe. Days before workmen mounted a 30-pounder Parrott gun and two

Paperwork regarding the naming and renaming of ships flooded the desk of U.S. Secretary of the Navy Gideon Welles. [LIBRARY OF CONGRESS]

12-pounder rifles upon the one-time merchant ship, she became the USS *Bigonia*.

In almost monotonous fashion, long-familiar names of purchased and captured vessels, many of them feminine, were scrapped— often in favor of flowers. Some of such changes were:

- *Heliotrope* instead of *Maggie Baker*
- *Acacia* in lieu of *Vicksburg*
- *Geranium* for *John A. Dix*
- *Violet* rather than *Martha*
- *Peony* for *Republic*
- *Jonquil* in lieu of *J. K. Kirman*
- *Fuchsia* instead of *Kiang Soo*
- First *Hornet* and then *Cuba* for *Lady Stirling*
- *Clarence* in lieu of *Coquette*
- *Albion* for *Lucy R. Waring.*

Some names of flowers bestowed upon vessels formerly bearing other titles include: *Gladiolus, Anemone, Hydrangea, Daisy, Jasmine, Pansy, Rose, Daffodil, Tulip, Periwinkle, Hollyhock, Dahlia, Primrose, Honeysuckle,* and even *Phlox.*

Imagine a tar-blackened seaman explaining to his wife or sweetheart that he was serving aboard the *Periwinkle* or the *Heliotrope!*

Numerous as they were, flowers accounted for only a fraction of new names for ships. Officials of the U.S. Navy selected many forts, generals, and battle sites when they renamed vessels. They also honored six states, eleven cities, and four birds—the petrel, curlew, oriole, and grossbeak.

Decades later this welter of double and triple names belonging to ships of every size and type remains a source of considerable confusion. It is apparent that the upper echelons of the U.S. Navy substituted many flower and animal names for those of women. In the process of having scores of vessels reregistered, they agreed to use only three feminine names: Pocahontas, Anna, and Emma.

A particularly puzzling change took place when the U.S. Navy acquired the bark *Abd-el-Kadir.* It's small wonder that the name was immediately changed, but records fail to indicate why the new Federal owners sent it to war as the USS *Ammonoosuo.*

Part Three

Notorious and Nonesuch

In sheer magnitude, the Civil War is in a class by itself. No other U.S. military involvement comes close to challenging its stupendous statistics. An estimated 623,000 Americans died during about 1,400 days of conflict. Only about one-third of them were combat fatalities, yet some or many who died took part in so many clashes that they lost count. Frederick H. Dyer, who devoted a great part of his life to compiling Union data, identified about 13,000 of these. Listed in order of diminishing size, they range from battles and engagements to actions and combats, sieges, skirmishes, affairs, reconnaissances, scouts, and "other military events." So many men and women took part in so many military and civilian affairs that ultimate achievements or events were inevitable.

Major Robert Anderson commanded the tiny garrison at Fort Sumter.
[ILLUSTRATED LONDON NEWS]

9

First Times

A majority of Confederate leaders and most of their foes in blue held that the first shot of the war was fired in Charleston Harbor on April 12, 1861. Lincoln, commander in chief of U.S. forces, had a different view. It was his contention that no state had actually seceded; although eleven claimed to have done so, according to the president, they were still in the Union. Traditionally, war was regarded as a conflict between two sovereign states. Since the independence of the Confederacy was not recognized, Lincoln termed the sectional struggle an insurrection. It came about, he said, by "a combination of forces too powerful to subdue by ordinary means."

So viewed, the April artillery duel between Federal and Confederate forces didn't start a war. Thus it was impossible to label the initial shell fired at Fort Sumter as having been first in the war.

Pennsylvania-born James Buchanan, Lincoln's predecessor in office, was adamant in his insistence that only Congress could declare war. He wasn't interested in a verbal subterfuge to justify sending troops to the South. More than anything else, Buchanan wanted peace. In a bid to secure that peace, Buchanan reluctantly endorsed the plans of his top military advisers. As a result, the merchant ship *Star of the West* was sent to Charleston Harbor with supplies and reinforcements for Maj. Robert Anderson and his tiny garrison at Fort Sumter.

Having received advance warning that the ship was en route, the Secessionists were prepared. When the vessel entered Charleston waters early on the morning of January 9, 1861, cadets from The Citadel military academy manning a battery on Morris Island, close to the Federal installation, placed a shot across the ship's bow. By many standards, that shot was the first of the war. The records are clear and precise; it was fired by Cadet George W. Haynesworth.

Full-scale military action would have followed this first shot in January had Lincoln, who was committed to the preservation of the Union at all costs, occupied the White House. Had that happened, Haynesworth would be much better known today.

Debate over the identity of the man who launched the first shell toward Fort Sumter began very early and has never completely subsided. Many of his admirers credited this honor to Edmund Ruffin of Virginia, an ardent Secessionist who went to Charleston hoping to participate in the fireworks. Much evidence suggests that Ruffin was offered the opportunity to begin the shelling, but he shook his head in refusal. Three or four other prominent Confederates have been identified as firing that first shot in April, but the evidence is inconclusive. An unidentified member of a Secessionist battery probably fired the shot that led Lincoln to try to put down an insurrection.

At least two members of the Fort Sumter garrison, both of whom later became prominent, claimed to have fired the first shot at a Confederate battery. Subsequently a brigadier, Jefferson C. Davis claimed that the honor belonged to him, but those comrades in arms who detested him discounted his report.

Career artillerist Abner Doubleday, then a captain, insisted that he was the first to fire upon Southerners who were trying to drive the Federal forces from Fort Sumter. After the conflict was over, Doubleday wrote a volume of *Reminiscences* in which he said the honor was indisputably his. Doubleday was made a major general in 1862, and his postwar book was widely circulated. Maybe because of these factors, the man who had nothing to do with the invention of baseball is usually identified as the first to return the Confederate fire.

If it was Doubleday and not Davis who fired the first shot from the Federal fort, it was a dud. Doubleday admitted, "My first shot bounded from the sloping roof of the battery opposite without producing any apparent effect." Regardless of how effective his fire may have been that day, he was promoted one month later, again on February 3, 1862, and once more just nine months later. After the 1863 battle of Gettysburg, Major General Doubleday was relieved of field duty and assigned to a desk job for the duration.

Abner Doubleday claimed to have fired the first Federal shot of the Civil War. [NATIONAL ARCHIVES]

No one has been identified as the person who fired the first shot at the first battle of Manassas (or Bull Run), but Confederate Brig. Gen. Richard S. Ewell is believed to have been the first to lead his men into battle there. According to his report, Ewell's brigade was made up of Robert E. Rodes's Fifth Alabama Infantry, John J. Seibels's Sixth Alabama, and Horatio Seymour's Seventh Louisiana. Four companies of cavalry and a battery of artillery accompanied the infantry.

On the morning of July 21, 1861, Ewell followed his orders to hold himself "in readiness to advance at a moment's notice." As a result, he and his men may have been first to arrive at what became the first major battleground of the war.

Confederate historians say that the first artillery shot at Manassas roared from the mouth of a 30-pounder Parrott gun at about 5:00 A.M. It is credited to a battery commanded by Capt. J. Howard Carlisle, who failed to record the name of the gunner.

The action at the first battle of Manassas was so chaotic that no one knows who may have fired the first shot. [FRANK LESLIE'S ILLUSTRATED NEWSPAPER]

Many persons interested in the largest of American wars think of Bull Run as being the first battle. Yet more than two weeks earlier, opposing infantry clashed at Philippi, Virginia (now West Virginia).

As battles go, this first encounter didn't amount to much. Federal forces attacked Confederates under Col. G. A. Porterfield just after daybreak on June 3. Outnumbered at least two to one and taken completely by surprise, Porterfield's men threw down their muskets and fled. The Confederates' departure from the first encounter between opposing troops was so rapid that the jubilant victors bragged that the skirmish constituted "the Philippi Races." That derisive label didn't last long, but while it was still current, Porterfield was censured and then relieved of his command.

Philippi put another first into the record books: after the battle, Pvt. Jim Hanger became the first man to have a leg amputated during the Civil War.

The clash at Philippi wasn't significant enough to be labeled a battle, and the bluecoats took a terrific beating at Manassas. Hence many analysts hold that the first Federal battlefield victory came at Mill Springs, Kentucky, little more than a year after cannon turned back the *Star of the West.* Part of the irony of the Union win lies in the fact that the Bluegrass State had officially declared itself to be neutral.

Some residents of the region in which the Confederates suffered their first significant defeat were not positive about its site. Many of them knew the place called Mill Springs, but most Federal records lists it as Logan's Cross Roads. Others believed that the battle in the neutral state occurred at Beech Grove, otherwise known as Sunset.

In his *Compendium of the War of the Rebellion,* Frederick H. Dyer—almost as well known for his conservative use of language as for his accuracy—listed the January 19, 1862, conflict as having occurred at Fishing Creek.

There's little or no debate about the fact that the first decisive Union victory in a pitched battle west of the Mississippi River was won at Pea Ridge, Arkansas. Confederates who admitted having been defeated there in March 1862 preferred to call the place Elkhorn Tavern.

Facts about the origin of baseball and the first shot fired from Fort Sumter are debatable, but there is no such discrepancy about Alexandria, Virginia. On May 24, 1861, Col. Daniel Butterfield of the Twelfth New York Militia led his men across Washington's Long Bridge before dawn. That made him the first Federal commander to set foot on Confederate soil during the hostilities. Throughout the North, the man remembered as the composer of "Taps" was hailed as a hero.

Many who joined in his praise conveniently forgot much that Lincoln had said in his First Inaugural Address. Speaking to the divided nation on March 4, 1861, the first Republican president said that the power of his office would be used "to hold, occupy, and possess the property, and places belonging to the government, and to collect the duties and imposts." Then he made a brief but solemn promise. Beyond doing what was necessary to accomplish these stated objectives, he said, "There will be no invasion—no using of force against, or among the people anywhere."

Less than two months later, that comment by the chief executive of the nation was exploded by artillery fire in faraway Charleston Harbor. As a result, Butterfield had the distinction of leading the first Federal troops to enter Virginia.

In the case of the soldiers in gray, the first invasion of enemy soil did not occur until September 5, 1862. It was neither planned nor led by Robert E. Lee. Troops under the command of Thomas J. "Stonewall" Jackson crossed the Potomac River at White's Ford, near Leesburg. Unlike the Federals who advanced upon Alexandria in silence, the confident Confederates sang at the top of their voices. The tune chosen by the first Southerners to enter Northern territory was "Maryland, My Maryland!"

Brig. Gen. Adam R. "Stovepipe" Johnson led the first successful Confederate invasion in the western theater. With only a handful of men, he penetrated Kentucky's Green River region south of Owensboro. So much alarm resulted from the 1862 raid that Indiana Gov. Oliver P. Morton sent an urgent telegram to Washington requesting more Federal cavalry be sent to the state immediately to prevent Johnson's crossing the Ohio River. Morton's plea for help arrived too late; Stovepipe and his ragged band had already struck at Newburgh, Indiana, and retired into Kentucky.

A few months earlier, Capt. Ezra Taylor of Battery B, First Illinois Light Artillery, filed the first official report of its kind. In it he reported a November 7, 1861, skirmish at Belmont, Missouri. Five men had been wounded; in each case, the rank and full name were given. Three horses were shot on the field, and two others sustained serious leg injuries.

Taylor's meticulous report, which reveals a great deal about the needs of a fighting force, then enumerated two sets of data always significant to a commander but seldom listed in detail:

> Left on the field: 2 caissons, 1 baggage wagon, 2 sets artillery lead harness, 1,000 ball cartridges for Colt's revolver, 200 rounds ammunition for 6-pounder guns, 25 double blankets, 20 canteens, 5 coats, 3 caps, 15 Colt's revolvers, 5 horse blankets, 6 sabers, 5 lanterns, 3 shovels, 1

overcoat, 2 currycombs and brushes, 2 fuse-gouges, 60 friction primers, 2 camp kettles, 20 cups, 1 leg guard, 1 sponge and rammer, 6 whips, 20 haversacks, 2 pick-axes, 4 felling axes, 1 trail handspike.

Captured from the enemy: 120 horses, 1 mule, 1 6-pounder brass gun, 1 12-pounder brass howitzer, and some fragments of artillery harness, and sundry small articles captured by individuals, not of any particular value to the service.

Taylor and his men went into action armed with four 6-pounder field guns, two 12-pounder howitzers with gun limbers and caissons complete. Guns and officers required 81 horses and 14 mules. Ammunition carried into the fight consisted of 1,000 rounds for guns and howitzers and 1,000 pistol cartridges. During the encounter, 114 Federal gunners fired 400 rounds on the field, lost 200, and returned from the action with 400.

In his *Compendium of the War of the Rebellion,* Frederick H. Dyer, who termed the meeting an "engagement," reported that six Federal units from Illinois and one from Iowa were also involved in addition to Taylor and Battery B: Dollins's Independent Cavalry Company; Delan's Adams County Cavalry; the Twenty-second, Twenty-seventh, Thirtieth, and Thirty-first Illinois Infantries; and the Seventh Iowa Infantry.

Dyer didn't attempt to compile Confederate statistics, and those who have made an effort to do so have found the records to be woefully lacking. Federal casualties included 80 killed, 322 wounded, and 99 missing.

Three days later, in another action, a man was leading troops despite the fact that his offer to serve the Union had been initially ignored. Having worn a blue uniform through the influence of the congressman whose district included Galena, Illinois, U. S. Grant had earlier "seen the elephant" in Mexico as a captain. Elihu B. Washburne's protégé experienced his first Civil War combat on Missouri soil, not far from Benton.

Confederates didn't win their first major victory in the West until September 1863. Their hour of glory came at Chickamauga, in southeastern Tennessee. Confederate Gen. Braxton Bragg failed to follow up his win and soon was so badly beaten at Chattanooga that he was removed from command.

The first major Confederate victory in the West was in 1863 at Chickamauga.
[HARPER'S WEEKLY]

Three weeks after Virginia had been invaded, men of seven Union regiments marched most of the night to reach the neighborhood of Great Bethel. Also called Big Bethel, Virginia, the region was known to have about twelve hundred Confederates under the command of Col. John B. Magruder.

An estimated twenty-five hundred Federals launched their attack under the command of Brig. Gen. Ebenezer W. Peirce. Although tiny by comparison with later clashes, the ensuing combat is often listed as the first battle of the war. When the dust settled, Magruder announced that the ratio of Federal to Confederate casualties was more than nine to one.

According to the *Confederate Military History*, Maj. Henry C. Carter of Richmond entered the record book at Great Bethel. He was credited with having fired the first cannon discharged during a "regular engagement" on Virginia soil.

At Gettysburg, the first battle in which more than forty thousand casualties occurred, the first shot is said to have been fired by Lt. Marcellus E. Jones of the Eighth Illinois Cavalry. For the record, the weapon he used was neither a musket nor a rifle, but a carbine, one of the standard weapons of Federal cavalry.

Henry Raison of the Seventh Tennessee Infantry is regarded as the first Confederate to die in the greatest of all American battles.

West Point graduate William T. Sherman, class of 1840, was in command of a brigade at Manassas in 1861. For the man destined to gain fame and infamy as the leader of the March to the Sea, the July battle constituted his first experience of combat.

During early action in Virginia's western region, now West Virginia, one of Sherman's opponents saw his first action of the Civil War. A professional soldier who had graduated from West Point in 1829 and had won slow advancement in the thirty-two years prior to the war, he did not achieve the rank of colonel until 1861.

Changing uniforms and accepting a new commission, Robert E. Lee led Virginia state forces at Conrad's Mill on September 11, 1861. It was at this remote point that he first commanded men under fire.

No longer a professional soldier without combat experience, Lee planned and executed the remainder of the Cheat Mountain campaign in western Virginia. His admirers sometimes fail to remember that this campaign ended in defeat for Lee's forces.

No pure cavalry engagement occurred until horsemen met at Kelly's Ford, Virginia, on March 17, 1863. This first battle of its sort resulted in only 211 casualties. One of them was Maj. John Pelham, called "as grand a flirt as ever lived" and nicknamed "the Gallant Pelham." In gratitude for his services, he received a posthumous promotion to the rank of lieutenant colonel.

Ten weeks after the action at Kelly's Ford, the largest cavalry battle in North America occurred at Brandy Station, Virginia. About ten thousand men on each side took part in the conflict that led to nearly one thousand Federal casualties and more than five hundred Confederate.

The impact of the battle was greater than these data suggest, however. Despite the losses by the soldiers in blue, Brandy Station demonstrated for the first time that Federal cavalry could fight as well as Confederates on horseback.

Reams Station, also in Virginia, was the point at which two battles took place. During the second one, Confederate Capt. Shade Wooten of North Carolina racked up a record that was never challenged.

Although the August 24–25, 1864, conflict produced more than three thousand casualties, Wooten was not among them. Three times he saved his life by throwing dirt at the eyes of a foe who was about to shoot him.

Alfred Ely of New York was the first sitting congressman to be captured in battle. Along with scores of other Washington celebrities, he couldn't resist riding out to see the action at Manassas Gap in July 1861.

While an inmate of Richmond's famous Libby Prison, Ely was picked for an especially demanding task. When the names of captured Federal officers were put into a hat, Ely drew them out one by one to determine which of them would become hostages for the safety of Confederate seamen threatened with death for the crime of piracy.

Brig. Gen. Robert S. Garnett achieved immortality of a sort by becoming the first general officer on either side to die of battle wounds. During a July 13, 1861, action at Corrick's Ford, Virginia (often identified as Carrick's Ford), the brigadier in blue was mortally wounded while attempting to withdraw his skirmishers from the field.

Garnett was by no means the first soldier to die. That honor went to Pvt. Daniel Hough of the First U.S. Artillery. According to Abner Doubleday, Hough was killed at Fort Sumter on April 14, 1861, when a cannon went off prematurely during a salute to the flag.

Purely accidental and not due to Confederate fire, the death was attributed to spongers who failed to extinguish fire inside the piece before it was reloaded. Hough's right arm was blown off, and he quickly bled to death.

Baltimore streets were darkened with blood when Union volunteers clashed with civilians. [HARPER'S HISTORY OF THE CIVIL WAR]

Hough wore the uniform of a regular in the U.S. Army. Just five days after his death, four ninety-day volunteers from Massachusetts were the first soldiers to die in combat—of a sort.

Marching through the streets of Baltimore, men of the Sixth Massachusetts were pelted with stones by pro-Secessionist civilians. A musket was fired, and men on both sides emptied their guns indiscriminately.

Pvts. Luther C. Ladd, Sumner Needham, Charles A. Taylor, and Addison O. Whitney were killed immediately or received mortal wounds. At least three times as many civilian residents of the Maryland city died as a result of the fray.

May 7, 1861, brought a first event of quite different nature. On that day an unidentified private in Company G of the Eighth New York Infantry carefully prepared his musket for action. He then sat down against a wall, rested his chin on the muzzle of his weapon, and

Elmer Ellsworth's Zouaves gained a reputation as a drill team prior to the war. Part of a romanticized view of combat, many Zouave units were formed early in the conflict. [LESLIE'S HISTORY OF THE CIVIL WAR]

tripped its flintlock. As a result he became the first Civil War soldier to die by his own hand.

Col. Elmer Ellsworth of the New York Fire Zouaves, or Eleventh New York Volunteers, was the first Federal commissioned officer to die. Ellsworth had just removed a Confederate flag from the roof of a hotel in Alexandria, Virginia, when the proprietor, James T. Jackson, shot him at close range on the stairway. Pvt. Francis E. Brownell promptly shot and killed Jackson.

So closely linked with Lincoln that he could be termed a favorite of the family of the commander in chief, Ellsworth's death caused the White House to be draped in mourning. Throughout the North he was lauded as a martyr for a righteous cause and labeled as "a war hero" despite the fact that he had never been in combat.

Capt. James H. Ward was the first Union naval officer to die in combat. As commander of the Potomac Flotilla, the twenty-eight-year veteran led an attack on Confederate batteries at the mouth of Aquia

Creek. During the artillery duel that followed, Ward took a direct hit and died immediately. His failed mission was designed to keep the river open and end the Confederate blockade of Washington. Records of the period are so chaotic that Ward's death is variously reported to have taken place on June 1, June 17, and June 27, 1861.

Shortly before or after Ward became a war hero, the name of Lt. John Greble of Company B, Second U.S. Artillery, went into the record books. One of the twenty-five hundred men who went to Big Bethel, Virginia, on June 9, 1861, under the leadership of Brig. Gen. Ebenezer W. Peirce, Greble became the first officer of the U.S. Army to die during the Civil War.

His battery had delivered only about a dozen rounds against the enemy before he was killed in action. Admirers saw to it that he received a succession of posthumous promotions that eventually catapulted him to the rank of lieutenant colonel.

Cyrus W. James of the Ninth New York Cavalry is listed as the first man to be killed at Gettysburg. He probably died not knowing that a cavalryman of the Eighth Illinois would be credited with firing the first shot and starting the largest battle of the war.

At Gettysburg, Federal Maj. Gen. John Reynolds was the first but not the last general to be killed or mortally wounded during the mammoth three-day struggle.

Albert Sidney Johnston, whose gray collar carried the three stars of a full general, was the first commander of an army to die in combat. While directing frontline operations at Shiloh, he was hit in the leg and bled to death before the wound was recognized as serious.

Only Maj. Gen. James B. McPherson was Johnston's counterpart of sorts in blue. Dropped by Confederates while on reconnaissance near Atlanta, the commander of the Army of the Tennessee died on the spot.

A little-known encounter took place two days before "the Philippi Races." John Q. (or R.) Marr, a Virginia Military Institute graduate, became captain of the Warrenton Rifles when he formed the unit.

Early one morning in June 1861, a few members of Company B, Second U.S. Cavalry, galloped through the village of Fairfax Court

At Aquia Creek, a ship-to-shore artillery duel brought about the first Union naval officer casualty. [VIRGINIA CAVALCADE]

House, Virginia. As they raced along the road, they fired a few shots at random. Struck in the chest, Marr became the first Confederate officer to die in combat.

Since both Fairfax Court House and Philippi were minor skirmishes, another name soon appeared on the roster of heroes in gray. Pvt. Henry L. Wyatt of Company A, First North Carolina Infantry, was felled by a Federal volley as the first battle of Manassas got under way. Consequently, he became the first Confederate soldier to die in battle.

While reconnoitering near Elkwater Bridge, Virginia, on September 13, 1861, Lt. Col. John A. Washington was killed. News of this tragedy in the mountains of Randolph County brought mourning to Virginia troops.

Washington, a long-time friend of Robert E. Lee, was the first member of his commander's family to die in combat. He fell early in Lee's fatally flawed first field campaign for the Confederacy.

Today several Civil War battlefields are heavily dotted with markers commemorating the men who fought there. Whether fashioned from granite or copper, these tributes are latecomers. A monument erected in September 1861 in memory of an Eighth Georgia Infantry officer was the first battlefield tablet erected for a fallen Civil War soldier.

CHAPTER

10

Claims to Fame

At least one out of every ten Confederate soldiers alive after Appomattox seems to have claimed to have been involved in the last gasp of the Lost Cause. Some of these doings show up in official documents, but many do not. Practically all of them have produced historical markers that were erected by state or local organizations. This subject is a challenge. To deduce the truth, the language used to describe a last military encounter has to be analyzed and the evidence sifted.

On December 6, 1911, Bvt. Maj. Gen. J. Warren Keifer of Ohio addressed a band of veterans. In his closing remarks he modestly indicated that his command was responsible for the capture of Robert E. Lee's oldest son. Powerfully built and standing six feet, two inches tall, Confederate Maj. Gen. George Washington Custis Lee was made a prisoner three days prior to his father's surrender to U. S. Grant.

Describing the capture of the high-ranking prisoner, Keifer said that it took place on April 6 "at Sailor's Creek, Virginia, the last field battle of the war."

No matter what terminology is used to label it, the fracas that occurred at Sayler's Creek was a lot more than a skirmish. Federal forces suffered about twelve hundred casualties before forcing nearly eight thousand men in gray to surrender.

Keifer was a colonel on April 18, 1865, when he compiled his official report at Burkeville, Virginia. In it he does not mention capturing Lee, saying only that the division of Custis Lee was "known to have participated in the battle."

Four days earlier at the same village, Pvt. Harris S. Hawthorn, Company F, 121st New York Volunteers, appeared before Judge

Advocate H. E. Hindmarsh of the First Division, Sixth Corps, to sign a sworn statement. According to it, Hawthorn was "the first person [officer or enlisted man] who seized or captured General Custis Lee, of the Confederate Army, in the engagement of the 6th of April."

His regiment, known as the Orange and Herkimer, was attached to the Second Brigade, First Division, Sixth Corps. When Lee was captured during the "last field battle," Keifer was a brevet brigadier at the head of the Second Division, Sixth Corps.

Three days after Sayler's Creek, with the surrender ceremonies at Appomattox having been completed, fierce fighting was under way near Mobile, Alabama. Forces under Edward R. S. Canby, a major general of U.S. Volunteers, attacked Fort Blakely at 5:30 P.M. on April 9.

Ranks of defenders included a brigade of boy reserves charged with holding the Confederate right flank. When attacked by sixteen thousand men in blue, they withered under fire and surrendered after twenty minutes of fighting. Federal casualties were about six hundred, but Canby considered that a small price to pay for thirty-four hundred prisoners and more than forty captured guns.

Confederate Maj. Gen. Richard Taylor commanded the Department of East Louisiana, Mississippi, and Alabama at the time of the capitulation at Blakely. Five days earlier he had decided to accept the surrender terms offered by Canby. Hence he met the Federal commander at Citronelle, Alabama, on May 4, to make the agreement official.

It wasn't until May 8 that paroles offered to his men were accepted, so Taylor insisted that the surrender occurred on that day. He consistently described it as "the surrender of the last major Confederate force east of the Mississippi River."

More than a month later, at Palmito (or Palmetto) Ranch on the Rio Grande, five hundred Confederates under Brig. Gen. James E. Slaughter fought against a band of sixteen hundred soldiers in blue.

Texas Rangers, whose commander was known as Rip Ford, made a futile charge at what survivors described as "a headlong gallop." On the Federal side, most of the fighting was done by men under the command of Col. T. H. Barret. To his dying day, Barret

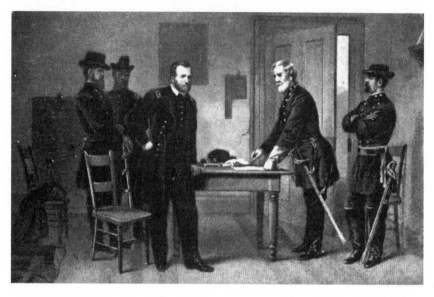

An unusual portrayal of the surrender ceremonies at Appomattox, this engraving was prepared by an artist who was not there. [VICTORY AT LAST! 1865]

insisted that his Sixty-second U.S. Negro Regiment took the honors in the last battle of the war.

Based partly upon Barret's claim, the death of Pvt. John J. Williams is regarded as the last Union combat fatality. A member of the Thirty-fourth Indiana Infantry, he fell before Confederates claimed victory on May 13, 1865.

Survivors of the struggle at Bentonville, North Carolina, scoffed at claims originating far to the west. On March 19, 1865, they were waiting for Federal troops to make a move and were delighted to see Maj. Gen. Henry W. Slocum's Army of Georgia in the distance.

The Confederates made three separate assaults in a struggle that ended after sunset, but they were repelled each time. Union officers failed to compile a careful tabulation of the casualties. Two days later, another clash at Bentonville was recorded as a Federal victory.

As a result, many authorities describe the North Carolina conflict as being "the last significant Confederate effort to halt Sherman." Confederate Lt. Gen. Wade Hampton, the Southern authority most often quoted, called Bentonville the "last general battle."

Although an estimated 2,650 Confederates were captured at Bentonville, there was no formal surrender of a major body of troops. That made it possible to erect a historical marker near the western edge of the state. The plaque reads:

> NEAR THIS SPOT
> THE LAST SHOT OF THE WAR
> BETWEEN THE STATES
> WAS FIRED UNDER THE COMMAND OF
> LT. ROBERT T. CONLEY
> OF THE CONFEDERATE ARMY
> MAY 6, 1865
> ERECTED BY
> UNITED DAUGHTERS OF THE CONFEDERACY
> OF THE DISTRICT OF NORTH CAROLINA
> 1892

A freestanding bronze tablet on South Main Street in Waynesville bears the message:

> GEN. JAMES G. MARTIN'S ARMY
> OF WESTERN NORTH CAROLINA,
> LAST CONFEDERATE FORCE IN
> THE STATE, SURRENDERED HERE
> ON MAY 6, 1865.

Regionally famous, Martin's "surrender" took place on the day Jefferson Davis moved south from Sandersville, Georgia, knowing that Federal cavalry were closing in on him.

In the contest for the honor of being the last to surrender, Confederate Gen. Edmund Kirby-Smith disputed any claims made by others who fought in gray. His Trans-Mississippi Department had been cut off from Richmond by the 1863 fall of Vicksburg, hence the area had become known as "Kirby Smithdom."

Kirby-Smith led his forces to Galveston late in May and reached a tentative surrender agreement with Federal leaders. On June 2, 1865, formal surrender ceremonies took place, after which he claimed to be the last Confederate general officer to surrender and then left the country for Mexico.

Stand Watie, however, seems to have the stronger claim to be the last Confederate general to surrender. Watie fought at Pea Ridge,

Edmund Kirby-Smith was among the last Confederate officers to surrender at war's end. [LIBRARY OF CONGRESS]

Arkansas, as a Confederate colonel of the Cherokee Mounted Rifles and took part in numerous engagements late in the war. On May 8, 1864, he became the only Native American to receive a commission as a Confederate brigadier.

Soon after learning that Lee had surrendered, Watie took to the hills. More than thirteen months after his elevation in rank, on June 23, 1865, Watie surrendered to Federal authorities.

Months earlier, Federal Maj. Gen. John M. Palmer faced what he considered to be a unique situation in Kentucky. Trying to get the better of irregulars, or bushwhackers, he put Edwin Terrill at the head of a band he described as "Federal guerrillas."

Terrill and his ragged followers were responsible for the May 1864 capture of William C. Quantrill. Some of the men who had followed Quantrill from Kansas escaped and successfully eluded their pursuers for months. Fourteen weeks after Appomattox, they rode into the outskirts of Louisville and handed over their weapons. Many residents of both Kansas and Kentucky insist that

William C. Quantrill was perhaps the best-known western guerrilla leader. [KANSAS STATE HISTORICAL SOCIETY]

these men, whose names were not preserved, were the last Confederates to surrender.

Archibald H. Thomson of the Twelfth Ohio Infantry would have scoffed at others who claimed to have effected the last capture of Confederates. At Sweetwater, Tennessee, he thought he had only one more job: completion of the final muster rolls. Suddenly he was ordered to lead twenty-five men to Chattanooga to collect some cattle belonging to the government.

On or about August 17, 1865, Thomson was told that the cattle had been stolen by a band of irregular Confederates whose leader was known only as Gatewood. Moving toward the region, the Federals were ambushed.

Thomson later said that he confronted the Confederates with nothing but a revolver. When he raised his weapon, twenty-five carbines were leveled on the gang. The guerrillas surrendered without a fight.

According to Thomson, the Federal exploit in Tennessee ended the war, since he was convinced that he had gained the last surrender of a Confederate force.

Maj. Aaron P. Brown of the Georgia State Militia saw things differently, of course. He was the surgeon in charge of a field hospital at Upson, and the stream of sick and wounded men diminished only slightly after Appomattox.

Brown continued to perform surgery and to administer laudanum and other drugs until a band of Federal cavalry entered the village where the doctor was still in uniform. They surrounded his tiny hospital and leveled their weapons. According to Brown, he regarded it as futile to resist, so he gave up his patients to the men in blue. The physician said, "My August 23, 1865, capitulation against overwhelming odds constituted the last surrender of Confederate troops."

CHAPTER
11

Distinctively Obscure

Observers on the bank of the Tennessee River could hardly believe their eyes. An immense fleet, known to be under the command of U. S. Grant, was moving in the direction of a site soon to become memorable—Shiloh.

An awed Confederate managed later to make a list of the names of the vessels. He found it to include 14 armed river boats and 153 steamboats of every imaginable size and build. T. M. Hurst insisted that nothing in history equaled this fleet. Even the Spanish Armada, he said, did not exceed it in number. According to Hurst, the vessels of Grant's expedition "were not exceeded in tonnage by any flotilla that ever broke the foam."

Both the USS *Lexington* and the USS *Tiger*—believed to be the first gunboats ever to appear on the Tennessee River—were included in the Federal fleet. In addition, according to Hurst, one vessel had a unique asset. Only the little steamer *Glendale* was equipped with a calliope.

Unique maritime events abounded, and many of them took place upon the rivers of the South. Lt. F. S. Conover, commander of the USS *Isaac P. Smith,* chafed at being assigned to patrol the Stono River near Charleston. Bored with running up and down the tiny waterway, his men drew a crude figure of a Confederate soldier and placed it on Johns Island to use for pistol practice.

Barely half a mile from the improvised pistol range, Confederates were enraged at seeing the improvised target. Late in January 1863, under cover of darkness, they managed to haul at least four guns close to the bank of the river.

Maj. Charles Alston concealed his battery under a huge live oak tree. From this concealment, on January 30, the Confederates opened fire upon the heavily armed Federal vessel. Return fire raked the hidden position as the vessel increased speed to remove itself from the range of the Confederate guns.

Carefully directed fire from shore, combined with luck, caused three hits to the boilers of the Federal vessel. Hopelessly disabled, the *Isaac P. Smith* became the only warship to surrender to a field battery. Within weeks, the 453-ton warship joined Confederate vessels in the defense of Charleston.

Every man aboard the CSS *Arctic* knew that she was a huge floating battery rather than a warship. When completed on November 30, 1863, the iron-plated monster mounted only three guns. Yet she entered the record books as the only Confederate vessel to have more than six hundred names on her muster roll. Despite her formidable manpower, the *Arctic* became useless when Wilmington, North Carolina, fell to Federal forces in 1865.

One month after the fall of Fort Sumter, a lookout aboard the screw steamer USS *Mohawk* (earlier the *Caledonia*) spotted an unusual vessel. Obviously so heavily loaded that it could not move rapidly, the large bark seemed to be headed for Key West.

Hailed, the ship proved to be the slaver *Wildfire*. Conveyed to New Orleans after it quickly surrendered, the vessel with a cargo of almost five hundred Africans was the only ship of its kind to be captured during the war.

Also in a class by itself, the *Hattie* was a vessel of quite different character. During her brief life, this blockade-runner made at least sixty successful runs. No other blockade-runner even came close to evading pursuers as many times.

Despite Confederate awe at the size of Grant's Tennessee River fleet, a long-standing Federal record was set in the eastern theater. At the age of thirty-six, Maj. Gen. George B. McClellan showed far more daring upon water than upon land. Having determined to move the Army of the Potomac from Washington to the peninsula of Virginia, he commandeered every available ship. In March 1862, his troops successfully landed and began a campaign that came within miles of Richmond. Castigated by Lincoln for having "the slows," McClellan's swift movement constituted the largest movement of troops by water until immense Allied fleets were assembled for action during World War I.

Confederates never came close to assembling an amphibious force the size of McClellan's army. Yet the self-styled independent nation that launched a war before acquiring a navy achieved rare distinction. Thousands of vessels took part in the four-year struggle. Of them, only the 790-ton cruiser *Shenandoah* succeeded in circumnavigating the globe while millions were fighting on land.

A sister vessel's impact was even more significant than the achievements of the Confederate raider. She is famous for having fought the *Monitor* to a draw in the world's first engagement between ironclads. Many an admirer of the CSS *Virginia* didn't know that she was the only famous warship to be built from a wreck that had been earlier burned almost to the water line.

Income from revenue collected at ports of entry was vital to the United States until 1861. That's why the Revenue Service had its own fleet of twenty-four vessels. Of these, the *Harriet Lane* was in a class by itself. She was the only side-wheel steamer used prior to the war to collect duties on imported goods.

Hundreds of armed vessels operated on the high seas, in rivers, and in harbors. Only one warship was stationed in the Great Lakes, however. Rated at 582 tons, the side-wheel steamer USS *Michigan* plowed through the waters of Lake Erie on a regular schedule.

Her armament consisted of a single gun that was considered adequate. Late in February 1865, however, U.S. naval authorities decided that the firepower of the lone patrol boat was inadequate. With the conflict nearly over, the *Michigan*'s battery was enlarged by a 30-pound Parrott rifle, five 20-pound rifles, six 24-pound guns, and two 12-pounders.

Launched at Erie, Pennsylvania, in 1844, the only Civil War vessel of its kind, renamed *Wolverine*, was still operating in 1915.

Coxswain John Cooper of the USS *Brooklyn* was the target of a hail of Confederate fire during the battle of Mobile Bay. He fought with such conspicuous bravery that he was awarded the Medal of Honor.

When he was subsequently assigned to shore duty, the building in which Cooper worked caught fire. Wind blew the flames into

The Shenandoah *was the last Confederate vessel to surrender.*
[OFFICIAL NAVAL RECORDS]

other structures, some of which held stockpiles of ammunition. Aware that a wounded soldier was likely to burn to death, Cooper raced through exploding shells to rescue him.

Again he received the Medal of Honor, becoming the only member of the U.S. Navy to receive two such decorations.

David D. Porter launched his maritime career at the age of eleven and, following the capture of Vicksburg, rose to the rank of rear admiral in 1863. As commander of the North Atlantic Blockading Squadron, Porter was a key figure in successive Federal assaults against Fort Fisher, North Carolina. When the last big installation of its sort surrendered, Admiral Porter received the Thanks of Congress for his victory. Earlier exploits had earned him two citations of this sort, making him the only officer of the U.S. Navy to be thanked formally by Congress on three separate occasions.

Numerous one-and-only records were scored on land. Although many towns and cities were besieged, only one large Union army was bottled up by the Southerners. Having withdrawn into Chattanooga in 1863, Federal forces were cut off for many days from their sources of reinforcement and supply.

Woodlawn National Cemetery at Elmira, New York, is believed to be the only site in the nation where fighting men in both blue and gray lie in a mass grave. Seventeen members of the Federal Eleventh Veteran Reserve Corps are buried there, along with about fifty Confederates. Men who were wearing gray at the time of their death came from at least eight North Carolina regiments, six Virginia units, and six Georgia regiments.

How did so many dead soldiers from such diverse units wind up in New York? On July 15, 1864, the worst railroad accident in U.S. history up to that time occurred near Shohola, Pennsylvania. An Erie Railroad head-on collision took the lives of all but one of thirty-seven men on a prison train.

All seventeen Union soldiers who died were serving as guards. Each of them was buried in his own coffin, probably fashioned from the wood of the wrecked railroad cars. The prisoners didn't fare so well; big but crude boxes were built to hold four bodies each.

An elaborate monument stands near the burial trench, at least seventy-five feet long, in which blue and gray uniforms were intermingled. Scanty records make it impossible to know whether or not the names chiseled in stone—Union on one side of the marker, Confederate on the other side—are accurate.

Records concerning Richmond's Chimborazo Hospital are both accurate and detailed. Once it was completed, it was years before any other medical facility challenged it for first place in size.

Spread over an estimated 120 acres, at its peak Chimborazo included nearly 200 buildings. Since 150 of these were medical wards, the Confederate institution could house 4,800 sick and wounded men.

At its peak the U.S. Military Telegraph Service used hundreds of men. Only one of them, J. C. Van Duzer, is mentioned in the record as having been a combat officer.

A view of a few buildings that made up Richmond's Chimborazo Hospital.
[MUSEUM OF THE CONFEDERACY]

Col. Anson Stager, head of the telegraph service, once received a confidential message from Van Duzer. According to it, Maj. Gen. U. S. Grant had ignored traditional lines of authority when he appointed an aide for Stager without consulting the colonel.

Soon learning that someone had challenged the appropriateness of his appointment, Grant quickly identified Van Duzer as the culprit and ordered him to a guardhouse. Civilian telegraph operators threatened to walk off the job unless Van Duzer was released. Grant broke up the strike by ordering close confinement for any man guilty of "contumacious conduct."

Since the squabble revolving around Van Duzer involved civilian employees, the matter could not be classified as mutiny. Yet the only combat officer of the U.S. Military Telegraph Service was applauded by his comrades as the only man to defy Grant and escape severe punishment.

After reaching its maturity, the U.S. Army Signal Corps was often regarded as a rival to the telegraph service. Not so at its beginning, however.

Maj. Albert J. Myer, who entered the U.S. Army as an assistant surgeon, became a signal officer on June 27, 1860. His new post was created especially for him by Congress, and after the appointment he found himself to be the only member of the corps.

U.S. Brig. Gen. Justus McKinstry's distinction—if that is the right label to confer upon him—was quite different in nature. He was the only general to be dismissed from the service for mishandling funds.

An 1838 graduate of West Point, he had an unblemished record of twenty-two years of military service. Because he could move beyond his peacetime rank by transferring into the U.S. Volunteers, he took that step on September 2, 1861.

As chief quartermaster in the Department of the West, McKinstry was responsible for purchasing huge quantities of food, uniforms, and supplies. Many with whom he dealt had little interest in the conflict except as an opportunity for easy money. Some of these manufacturers and dealers specialized in "shoddy," the term used for blankets, tents, and garments made from cloth that quickly deteriorated in use. One such dealer with whom McKinstry did much business, the firm of Child, Pratt, and Fox, reaped a windfall of just under $1 million in a matter of months.

Accused of having lined his own pockets by purchasing huge quantities of shoddy, McKinstry was arrested, tried, convicted, and cashiered in 1863.

Camp Chase, near Columbus, Ohio, was the site at which a regiment was organized very early. Mustered into service on June 11, 1861, men of the Twenty-third Infantry left for Benwood, Virginia (now West Virginia), on July 25.

By war's end, the regiment had participated in scores of actions, ranging from a minor skirmish at Cross Lane, Virginia, on August 26, 1861, to South Mountain and Antietam.

When veterans were mustered out on July 26, 1865, every man of the regiment knew that relatives and descendants would be proud of him. What they could not foresee was that of the multitude of regiments in the Union army, only the Twenty-third Ohio Infantry included two future presidents: Rutherford B. Hayes and William McKinley.

Numerous military departments under Federal control were merged with others or dissolved. Only one, the Department of Texas, was given to the Confederacy by its commander.

At a postwar clambake, President Rutherford B. Hayes bore little resemblance to a Civil War officer. [LIBRARY OF CONGRESS]

Brig. Gen. David E. Twiggs, a distinguished veteran of the Mexican War, was strongly sympathetic to the Southern cause. Known to many of his officers as "the Bengal Tiger," he repeatedly requested instructions from Washington during the early weeks of 1861.

No orders came, so on February 18 the Tiger engaged in a brief ceremony with Col. Ben McCulloch, commander of Confederate troops in Texas. Twiggs formally turned over every fort and outpost in the department, along with two thousand soldiers, all of his equipment, and all U.S. Army funds on hand.

By May 22 the long-time veteran of Federal fighting forces was wearing the uniform of a Confederate major general, having been dismissed from Union service twenty-one days earlier. Twiggs was the oldest and most senior U.S. Army officer to switch uniforms. He also was the only Federal brigadier to surrender to Confederates substantially more than 10 percent of all men in the U.S. Army.

James J. Andrews is believed to have been born in Finland and to have been named Andreas Johan Kars. He probably fought in the Russian army before coming to Kentucky about 1850. Experienced in undercover work—or capable of convincing others that he was experienced—Andrews became a spy for the Union.

In 1862 he devised a plan to disrupt the flow of goods from Georgia into the other Confederate states. At the head of twenty-two Ohio soldiers who volunteered for the mission, he tried to cut the Western and Atlantic Railroad. Rainy weather and an exceptionally persistent railroad conductor foiled his plans. He and many of his men were captured; several were executed, but the survivors were among the first recipients of the Medal of Honor.

Andrews became the only civilian raider to be remembered because of failure.

North Carolina's Fort Fisher was a tempting target as 1865 began. A December expedition led by U.S. Maj. Gen. Benjamin F. Butler fizzled before it could gain the fort, leaving the port of Wilmington as the Confederacy's last gateway to England and Europe.

Frustrated, Lt. Gen. U. S. Grant established a special eight-thousand-man "provisional corps" headed by Brig. Gen. Alfred H. Terry. Terry's only assignment was to take Fort Fisher.

Given a free hand to assault or besiege the Southern fortification, Terry persuaded naval authorities to put more than fifty warships at his disposal. Since they were armed with at least six hundred guns, their bombardment was expected to weaken the Confederate defenses and facilitate an amphibious landing.

For the first few hours on January 12, things went according to plan. With the warships firing as rapidly as possible, thousands of men landed on the beach just south of Wilmington. In an all-out assault on January 15, hand-to-hand combat lasted for hours.

At the height of the frenzied fighting, the Ninety-seventh Pennsylvania Regiment was the first to plant its flag on the Confederate parapet. Col. Galusha Pennypacker, commander of the forces that included the Ninety-seventh, received a nearly fatal wound while personally accompanying the flag.

Pennypacker was immediately given a brevet as a brigadier and was formally promoted to that rank a month later. This action, which required congressional sanction, made the man from the Keystone State the youngest general officer in blue. When the new brigadier general celebrated his birthday in June, he "achieved his majority," that is, he was twenty-one years old and then eligible to vote.

Isaac Murphy was never quite sure how he came to be chosen as a delegate to a special convention held in Arkansas. He'd been a surveyor, teacher, lawyer, and was one of the multitude who had gone to California during the gold rush. Regarded by friends and neighbors as "uncommonly outspoken," he had made no secret of his allegiance to the Union.

At the call of the governor, a secret session of the convention convened on May 6, 1861. With seventy members present, sixty-nine voted in favor of the ordinance of secession. Undaunted, Murphy refused to budge from his position and cast his lone vote against the measure. His action made him the only documented member of a Southern convention who openly defied every other delegate.

Early in April 1864 the Federal Army of the Potomac appeared stymied. Plans called for movement across the James River near Wyanoke Landing. At this point the river was about twenty-one hundred feet wide. Tidal currents had cut some channels to a depth of fifteen fathoms. To amateurs and veterans alike, it seemed impossible to devise a way by which tens of thousands of men could cross the water.

Maj. J. C. Duane, an experienced pontonier, was put in charge of a handpicked crew of 450 army engineers. Assisted by Capt. G. H. Mendell, Duane sketched a temporary bridge that would be supported by three schooners. The materials were assembled and the plans completed, but work did not start until orders were received just before noon on June 15.

With the first schooner anchored and two others moving toward strategic spots, Duane started putting pontoons together. By using 101 of them, he managed to reach the opposite shore of the river

Skilled pontoniers could effect a river crossing in a few hours. [HARPER'S HISTORY OF THE CIVIL WAR]

in eight hours. No other pontoon bridge built during the conflict came close to this one in length.

The crossing of the army was completed early on the morning of June 18. When every man was over, the only improvised bridge of the war to exceed two thousand feet in length was broken into three sections. Treated as rafts, the sections were floated to Grant's headquarters at City Point, Virginia.

From his pulpit in Brooklyn, New York, Henry Ward Beecher vigorously denounced slavery. Translating words into action, he raised funds that enabled opponents of slavery to move to Kansas, where settlers would decide whether to form a free or a slaveholding state.

Violence erupted in the territory early in the 1850s and mounted in intensity as the years passed. Generally known as Bleeding

Henry Ward Beecher, an abolitionist, shipped rifles to prewar Kansas in crates marked Bibles. [NEW YORK PUBLIC LIBRARY]

Kansas, it was in this territory that John Brown perpetrated a massacre and developed his plans to create a new nation of former slaves.

In distant Brooklyn, Beecher found more and more persons willing to underwrite the antislavery movement in Kansas. Positive documentation is lacking, but the evidence confirms that wagonloads of crates were shipped west marked "Beecher's Bibles." Since many or all of these shipments contained rifles, the action made Beecher the lone prominent clergyman to fight slavery with the most advanced weapons money could buy.

Maj. Innis N. Palmer of the renowned U.S. Second Cavalry had no idea that his name would go into record books on July 21, 1861. He only knew that his provisional battalion of seven cavalry companies drawn from three regiments was expected to drive the Confederates from the Manassas battlefield.

When the day ended and the Federal forces were in full flight back to Washington, Brig. Gen. Irvin McDowell, who had been a major three months prior, discovered that Palmer's men had been his entire cavalry force at Manassas. As a reward for being the only leader of Federal mounted units in the first real battle of the war,

At Manassas, the first major battle of the war, in 1861, Gen. Irvin McDowell had only one unit of cavalry. [LIBRARY OF CONGRESS]

Palmer was given a brevet promotion. Two months later the honorary rank was made permanent and Brigadier General Palmer led brigades to Yorktown, Williamsburg, and Seven Pines.

Godfrey Weitzel of Ohio, an 1855 graduate of West Point, chafed at the slow promotion rate that characterized the army in time of peace. Although the outbreak of war brought a host of rapid promotions, he failed to gain advancement. As a result, he transferred to the U.S. Volunteers in August 1862 and was made a brigadier. Within two years he was Major General Weitzel, USV.

One month after achieving that rank, Weitzel was given command of the newly organized Twenty-fifth Corps. His men were the first Federals to enter Richmond in 1865 after the Confederate capital was abandoned. That was enough to make his name honored in the North and despised in the South. The intensity of sectional reaction was heightened by the fact that Weitzel headed the only corps of African Americans in the U.S. armed forces.

Pvt. Henry Brown of Darlington, South Carolina, is renowned as having been the only regularly enrolled man of African descent who

Seeking rapid promotion in 1842, Godfrey Weitzel transferred from the regular army to the U.S. Volunteers.
[REBELLION RECORD]

fought in the Confederate forces of his state. Brown was not issued a musket or rifle; he carried a drum.

Since his combat service was in a class by itself, South Carolina citizens later decided to extend to him another unique honor. A monument fifteen feet tall was erected to his memory, the only memorial of its sort in the Old Confederacy.

Confederate Maj. Gen. Earl Van Dorn fought throughout two years of war without achieving special distinction on the battlefield. Fame of a sort came to the Mississippi native after he moved his division into Middle Tennessee, where he discovered a particularly charming young woman living in Spring Hill.

Soon the 1842 graduate of West Point was seen in the village and at his camp with the Maury County woman he found fascinating. She proved to be the moving force behind events that gave the Confederate officer a unique distinction. On May 7, 1863, he died, not in battle, but from a single shot delivered by Dr. George B. Peters. The action by the Tennessee physician made Van Dorn the only general officer of the Civil War to be killed in uniform by a jealous husband.

While proudly wearing his gray uniform, Pvt. Edward D. White was one of thousands captured by the Federals during the Vicksburg campaign. When he surrendered at Port Hudson, there was nothing unusual about the fact that he was required to give his parole not to resume fighting until regularly exchanged.

White would today be forgotten were it not for the fact that he exchanged his regular garb for a black robe thirty years after the end of the war. When he took his oath of office, the man from Louisiana's La Fourche Parish became the only former prisoner of war to serve as an associate justice of the U.S. Supreme Court.

Debate concerning the origin of the familiar nickname bestowed upon Confederate Brig. Gen. Thomas J. Jackson is not likely to subside. No one knows for certain what Brig. Gen. Barnard Bee meant when he said that Jackson stood "like a stone wall" at Manassas. Earlier, as an instructor at the Virginia Military Institute, the

Federal forces enter Richmond on the heels of the Confederate evacuation.
[LIBRARY OF CONGRESS]

man who became immortalized as Stonewall had been called Old Blue Light and Tom Fool.

Bee's comment may have been a compliment, but some suggest it was an insult. Whatever the case, after July 21, 1861, "Old Blue Light" was forgotten as "Stonewall" scored victory after victory. From that day on the Manassas battlefield to the end of the war, his brigade was known officially as the Stonewall Brigade. That made it the only brigade in gray to be designated by an officer's nickname.

George W. Johnson of Kentucky, a plantation owner and attorney, scoffed when the state's elected leaders announced that the state would be neutral in the sectional struggle. He sought and won election as the first head of the provisional Confederate government established by the Bluegrass State.

Chafing at civilian life while the fighting was escalating, Johnson volunteered his services to Confederate Gen. Albert Sidney Johnston. Enrolled as an adviser without a uniform, he was later transferred to the staff of Maj. Gen. John C. Breckinridge.

Johnson accompanied the former vice president of the United States to the battlefield at Shiloh, where a horse was shot from under him early in the struggle. Demanding an opportunity to fight rather than to advise, within hours he enlisted as a private in the First Kentucky Infantry.

Private Johnson was struck during his first day of fighting and died on April 9. Had he known of his unique niche in the story of the Civil War, he would have smiled at the honor of being the only governor to die of Civil War battlefield wounds.

French-born Victor Jean Baptiste Girardey, reared in Georgia and Louisiana as an orphan, hurried to enlist when Jefferson Davis called for volunteers. By October 1861 he was a lieutenant and became a captain just three months later.

Captain Girardey fought during the Seven Days battles and at Chancellorsville and Gettysburg without special distinction. His moment came at Petersburg, where he acted without orders and led two brigades in resisting Union forces in the battle of the Crater.

Girardey's Petersburg exploit was brought to Lee's attention, and the general saw to it that the native of France received a third promotion. This time, he became the only Confederate to jump four ranks—from captain to brigadier general.

Hundreds of clergymen left their flocks to go to the battlefield with the units mustered from their villages and towns. Most of them served faithfully in obscurity.

Not so the Reverend T. L. Duke of the Nineteenth Mississippi Regiment. Near Fredericksburg, Virginia, men of Brig. Gen. Carnot Posey's brigade wavered during hand-to-hand fighting. Duke seized a musket, raced to the front of his regiment, and there "mainly directed the movements of the skirmishers."

As a result, the Mississippi clergyman became the only Confederate chaplain to be cited officially for gallantry in battle.

12

One of a Kind

When President Lincoln called for seventy-five thousand volunteers to serve for ninety days, the response was immediate and overwhelming. As the conflict dragged on, however, Washington was forced to adopt a system of conscription. Quotas were assigned to states, and individuals were chosen for service by means of a lottery, or "draft."

Tens of thousands of men who didn't want to go to war after having been drafted hired substitutes to take their places. Among those to do so was a Buffalo, New York, resident who later occupied the White House: Grover Cleveland. But Cleveland was not the first chief executive to hire a wartime substitute.

Although the action was a symbolic one, Lincoln hired a substitute to serve in his place. Unlike John D. Rockefeller and J. Pierpont Morgan, who also hired substitutes, the president was not subject to the draft. Lincoln never explained his action. Pennsylvania native John S. Staples accepted at least five hundred dollars—well above the normal rate—to put on a Federal uniform and fight as Lincoln's substitute.

Matthew Brady of New York is the best known Civil War photographer. After having tried to become a painter, he opened a daguerreotype studio. Specializing in portraits, he achieved enough success to establish a branch studio in Washington.

By the time Fort Sumter had been fired upon, Brady had developed a skill in the new wet-plate photographic process. Although extremely slow by today's standards, the use of wet plates was suitable for battlefield use. Hence the New Yorker hired a corps of assistants to follow Federal troops wherever they went.

Matthew Brady's photographers and their equipment wagons were at nearly every major battlefield. [AMERICAN MUSEUM OF PHOTOGRAPHY]

It is doubtful that Brady was responsible for any familiar images taken in the field; his sight was failing rapidly by 1861. Yet he put his name upon thousands of photographs taken by Timothy O'Sullivan, Alexander Gardner, and other photographers. As a result, more wartime images are credited to Brady than to any other photographer. Properly speaking, most of them should be credited to the Brady Studio.

New Hampshire native Benjamin F. Butler moved to Massachusetts and became a powerful figure in the Democratic Party. A successful criminal lawyer, he took command of Massachusetts Volunteers three days after Lincoln's call for volunteers following the debacle at Manassas Junction.

Within a month Butler was wearing two stars and is now remembered as having been the first of Lincoln's so-called political generals. Some analysts attribute his appointment to the president's political acumen; after all, a leading Democrat couldn't simultaneously fight Confederates and oppose Republicans at the polls.

Regardless of the factors that led the president to honor him, Butler soon became the only Union general to be condemned across Europe. International reactions stemmed from the most violent of several controversial actions. As military head of occupied New Orleans, he was the only Union general to order the execution of a civilian.

Shortly after New Orleans had surrendered, William B. Mumford, a professional gambler, tore down a U.S. flag that had been raised at the former U.S. Mint building and dragged it through the streets. When Butler's troops arrived to occupy the town, the general was informed of Mumford's actions and ordered the gambler's arrest. Tried and convicted of treason, Mumford was hanged on June 7, 1862.

Robert Anderson was praised as a national hero in the North, but Com. James Armstrong was branded as a traitor. Armstrong had served twenty-eight years in the navy when on May 29, 1861, the *New York Courier and Enquirer* called for his dismissal in disgrace.

Prior to Anderson's surrender of Fort Sumter, Armstrong had given up the U.S. Navy Yard at Pensacola, Florida, on January 12, 1861, without a struggle. At Charleston, victorious Secessionists told Anderson he was free to go where he pleased; at Pensacola, Armstrong became a captive.

Alone among naval officers of high rank, the New Jersey native had surrendered an important installation long before the outbreak of civil war. When released by his captors, Armstrong was court-martialed and suspended from duty. At war's end, the sole officer of his rank to be humiliated by Secessionists and Unionists alike was promoted to the rank of captain.

Relatives and acquaintances of Hinton R. Helper did not laud him during the time of tension that preceded the siege of Fort Sumter. In 1857 he financed the publication of a little book that he called *The Impending Crisis of the South: How to Meet It.*

Born and reared in North Carolina, he knew just enough about the North to realize that the sectional gap was immense and growing. To Helper, it seemed self-evident that the decisive difference between the two regions stemmed from the fact that the working population in the North was free, while a majority of workers in the South were enslaved.

Part of the paradox of the Tarheel's achievement stems from the fact that this southerner who condemned slavery was an avowed racist. His zeal for the abolition of slavery stemmed from an eagerness to help poor white laborers.

Chicago erected a huge meeting hall, The Wigwam, for the Republican National Convention of 1860. [HARPER'S WEEKLY]

Despite this factor, his book was received with enthusiasm in the North, where an estimated 14,500 copies were sold. With the election of 1860 approaching, the Republican National Committee printed and distributed about 100,000 copies of an abbreviated and expurgated version. Because Congressman John Sherman of Ohio endorsed much that Hinton had written, he was defeated in a contest for the vital post of Speaker of the House.

Another Republican political leader, William H. Seward of New York, gave a commendation of sorts to the Hinton volume, which is believed to have been a significant factor in his razor-thin defeat when members of his party gathered in Chicago to choose a presidential nominee. Motivated solely by economic considerations, the antislavery racist who vented his frustration by writing a book is the only author known to have helped put Lincoln into the White House.

An adopted son of Cmdr. David D. Porter, David G. Farragut received a commission as midshipman at age nine. Born in Tennessee, the career naval officer was living in Virginia when the war began. Many residents of Norfolk soon made it clear that a man

Wade Hampton of South Carolina distinguished himself on horseback during four years of the war. [MUSEUM OF THE CONFEDERACY]

known to harbor strong Unionist sentiments was not welcome in the port city.

Disgusted and angry, Farragut moved to the North, where he soon found that high-ranking officials were also suspicious of him because of his southern background. Porter, who insisted that his foster son was loyal, had the ear of the assistant secretary of the navy, Gustavus V. Fox. Together they persuaded the secretary of the navy, Gideon Welles, to give Farragut a chance. When the suspect captain was put in charge of the West Gulf Blocking Squadron, he soon captured New Orleans, the largest city in the Confederacy.

Two years later Farragut led Federal warships into Mobile Bay. Despite the presence of numerous floating mines, or torpedoes, he won a stunning victory. As a reward, the rank of vice admiral was created and awarded to him. In 1866 another new rank was established especially for Farragut, and he became the first full admiral in the nation's history. Not bad for a man whose loyalty had been questioned just five years earlier.

South Carolina plantation owner Wade Hampton had no military training or experience, but he was eager to fight. He raised volunteers who formed units of infantry, cavalry, and artillery that made up a hybrid organization known as Hampton's Legion.

Hampton's cavalry met George Armstrong Custer's brigade near Gettysburg on July 3, 1863. [AUTHOR'S COLLECTION]

Colonel Hampton was awarded the stars of a brigadier after ten months of service and became a major general in September 1863. His last promotion came sixty days before the surrender at Appomattox, after which he led Gen. Joseph E. Johnston's cavalry to resist Sherman's armies advancing through the Carolinas.

When the last major army in gray surrendered at Durham's Station, North Carolina, Hampton returned to South Carolina as the only Secessionist who was stripped of more than three thousand slaves as a result of the war.

Before Hampton began recruiting men for military service, numerous Southerners suffered other big losses. One after another, members of the House of Representative and the U.S. Senate gave up their seats. With the size of Congress greatly reduced, a man from Tennessee stubbornly clung to his place after his state seceded.

Because he became a conspicuous figure in Washington when his Southern colleagues went home, Andrew Johnson became well known to Lincoln. Picked as the running mate for the president who was seeking a second term, Johnson became chief executive following Lincoln's assassination. That forced him to preside over the early years of Reconstruction.

Had he not been notoriously stubborn, Johnson would not have remained in the Senate as its lone member from the South. This trait also caused him to become the only president to be impeached.

Long before that momentous event took place, he was the only future chief executive unable to write at the age of seventeen. A one-time apprentice to a tailor, Johnson acquired that skill from sixteen-year-old Eliza McCardle. They married on May 5, 1827, without dreaming that the eighteen-year-old bridegroom was going to the altar at an earlier age than any other future president.

London-born Edward D. Baker saw a political opportunity when statehood for Oregon was looming. Earlier he had been a member of the Illinois house of representatives and an organizer of the Republican Party in California. During his Illinois years he formed a close friendship with attorney Abraham Lincoln, so that the man from Springfield chose Edward as his second son's name.

Seated as a U.S. senator from Oregon late in 1860, Baker yearned for military service when war erupted. His friend in the White House offered to make him a brigadier, but he declined the commission because acceptance would have forced him to give up his seat in the Senate.

Late in the summer of 1861 the man from England, Illinois, California, and Oregon turned to Pennsylvania. When offered to become their colonel, the soldiers of the Seventy-first Pennsylvania Infantry, popularly known as the California Regiment, made it clear that they were itching to fight.

By this time Baker had received a major general's commission from Lincoln, which he neither accepted nor declined. Hoping for a brilliant military victory that would enhance his career, Colonel Baker blundered into a disastrous fight at Ball's Bluff, Virginia. On October 21, 1861, this ambitious wanderer and intimate of the president became the only sitting U.S. senator to die on the battlefield.

Another Federal colonel carved a niche for himself larger than that of Baker, but he never held political office. An inveterate inventor, mechanical engineer Hiram Berdan of New York City was considered by some northerners to be "thoroughly unscrupulous and unreliable."

Winslow Homer's "Sharpshooter" is among the most famous Civil War works of art. [LIBRARY OF CONGRESS]

Nevertheless, for a dozen years before the war he was touted as the top rifle shot in the United States. His fame was such that when the conflict began it was easy for him to recruit enough volunteers to fill two regiments, dubbed Berdan's Sharpshooters.

Colonel Berdan of the First U.S. Sharpshooters probably entered the recruitment business to develop new markets for his military inventions. His men could be identified at a glance; they wore green coats and green caps adorned with black plumes. Instead of carrying muskets, they were armed with .52-caliber Sharps rifles.

Officers and men who made up the body claimed, probably correctly, that they eliminated more Southern soldiers than any other force of comparable size. Especially proud of often silencing Confederate batteries with their powerful rifles, more than one thousand of the twenty-six hundred sharpshooters were killed or wounded during four years of constant action.

At Chancellorsville and at Gettysburg their leader went into battle at the head of a brigade. In the mellow mood of postwar generosity, Congress awarded two brevets to Berdan, brigadier general and major general.

Apparently initially motivated by the desire to make money from the sale of his inventions, Berdan did not succeed in that effort. Instead, the force he raised and led became one of the most memorable of those who wore, well, at least a bit of blue.

Although Henry M. Stanley found fame when he discovered David Livingstone in Africa, years earlier he had engaged in a series of actions that may have been without parallel. At the age of twenty and infected with "war fever," Stanley abruptly quit his job to enlist in the Sixth Arkansas Infantry. Along with numerous comrades captured at Shiloh, he was sent to a prison near Chicago.

Life at Camp Douglas was harsh, and there seemed to be no prospect of release. Hence the Confederate combat veteran became a "galvanized Yankee" by taking an oath of allegiance and exchanging his gray uniform for a blue one. Soon discharged because of illness, he went to New York and enlisted in the U.S. Navy. Stanley, also known as John Rowlands, is the only serviceman known to have served in the Confederate army, the Union army, and the U.S. Navy. His unique military career came to an end when he jumped ship at a New Hampshire port early in 1865 and became a deserter.

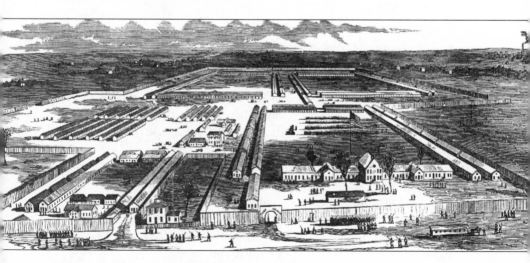

Camp Douglas Prison sprawled over many acres near Chicago. [HARPER'S HISTORY OF THE CIVIL WAR]

John C. Breckinridge of Kentucky helped to splinter the Democratic Party in 1860, keeping Stephen A. Douglas out of the White House and opening the door for Abraham Lincoln. [DICTIONARY OF AMERICAN PORTRAITS]

With 1860 seen as a crucial political year, Vice President John C. Breckinridge of Kentucky was a candidate for the presidency. Although he didn't come close to winning in November, he garnered more than 1.4 million popular votes. Eleven states gave him seventy-two electoral votes—almost one-fourth as many as Lincoln, because one American in sixteen voted for him.

In March 1861 he succeeded John J. Crittenden as a senator from Kentucky, but he resigned from the Senate to accept a brigadier's commission in the Confederate army. Promoted to major general in April 1862, he remained in uniform until February 4, 1865, when he became Confederate secretary of war. After the war, Breckinridge left the United States for three years, traveling to England and Canada. In 1868 he returned to Kentucky and practiced law for seven years, until his death in 1875.

Breckinridge's fame was of a sort that no other former vice president has matched, although Aaron Burr came close. He was the only former vice president to take up arms against the United States.

Jesse Bright's name seldom appears on any list of notable Civil War figures. In view of his record, that omission is remarkable.

Bright hailed from Indiana, where Lincoln spent many of his boyhood years. He was a state legislator and a lieutenant governor before going to Washington in 1845. During fifteen years in which he gained seniority, Bright three times served as president pro tem of the Senate, despite the fact that he had made numerous political enemies, some of whom were prominent in his own Democratic Party.

On December 16, 1861, lawmakers who sensed that something unusual was about to happen crowded into the chamber. A letter dated March 1, 1861, and written by Bright was read into the record. According to it, Bright's friend Thomas B. Lincoln had made a significant improvement in firearms. The letter would have stirred no interest had it not been sent to Montgomery, Alabama, and addressed to "His Excellency Jefferson Davis, President of the Confederation of States."

The fact that a U.S. senator had recognized the separate legal identity of the seceded states caused a turmoil in the Senate. Bright's colleagues devoted most of twenty working days to debate concerning the terse memorandum. Bright made a long and vigorous speech in his defense and found more supporters than his record would have caused him to expect.

In the end, the term "President Jefferson Davis" was too much for Bright's colleagues to accept. Repeatedly, the president of the United States had underscored his verdict that no secession had taken place. Bright was expelled formally in February 1862, the first senator to be removed by his colleagues.

Because he served for a decade as a Methodist circuit rider, William G. Brownlow was known as "Parson." Turning to another vocation, he founded a little newspaper known as the *Elizabethton (Tenn.) Whig*. Soon he took his publication to a larger city, where it became *Brownlow's Knoxville Whig*.

Through his journalistic pursuits, the former clergyman found an audience and a following. He made the most of his leadership opportunities when war broke out, planning and perhaps participating in the burning of several railroad bridges.

Driven from East Tennessee as a well-known bridge-burner, Parson Brownlow forayed into the North. Highly successful as a speaker at recruitment rallies, he sold an estimated one hundred thousand copies of a little book with a big title, *Sketches of the Rise, Progress, and Decline of Secession; with a Narrative of Personal Adventures Among the Rebels.*

When Union troops gained the advantage in East Tennessee, Parson Brownlow returned with the first wave of men in blue. He soon reestablished his newspaper as the *Knoxville Whig and Rebel* and at war's end became governor of the state.

Brownlow's most unusual claim to fame stems from his frequently announced views. No other chief executive of a former Confederate state was both an ardent supporter of the Union and a fiercely vocal opponent of the abolition of slavery.

Indiana-born Ambrose E. Burnside graduated from West Point in 1847 and was assigned to the artillery branch of the service. His Mexican War duties consisted only of garrison assignments, but he was later wounded while fighting Apaches in New Mexico.

During his recuperation he devised a way to improve breechloading carbines. His invention had such potential that he resigned from the army and became a weapons manufacturer in Rhode Island.

With the outbreak of the war, he became a major of the First Rhode Island Infantry on May 2, 1861—a command he held only one month. After having led a brigade at the battle of Manassas, Burnside accepted a brigadier's rank in the U.S. Volunteers.

His successful leadership of the North Carolina Expeditionary Corps (from December 1861 to April 1862) repeatedly put his name into headlines. Probably as a result of the publicity gained from his penetration into Secessionist territory, Lincoln offered to put the Hoosier at the head of the Army of the Potomac. Burnside declined, believing that he lacked adequate experience. When Lincoln's patience with George B. McClellan was exhausted following the battle of Antietam, the president again approached Burnside and made it clear that he expected immediate acceptance.

Perhaps reluctantly, Burnside took command over the most powerful Federal army in the country. Now remembered more for his facial hair than for his successes on the battlefield, Burnside's ineptness demonstrated that he—not Lincoln—was right about his ability to lead an army.

Veteran newspaper correspondent Sylvanus Cadwallader of the *New York Herald* wore a coonskin cap when he was attached to

Grant's forces in August 1862. Fellow journalists initially saw nothing special in Cadwallader, but within a year they discovered that he was one of the best of their vocation.

On Mississippi's Yazoo River, aboard the USS *Diligence* in June 1863, Cadwallader encountered a drunken Grant. He ushered the general to his stateroom and disposed of the commander's whiskey. Later aided by Col. John A. Rawlins, Cadwallader is credited with preventing Grant's dismissal.

His action earned Grant's appreciation and respect because Cadwallader refused to make anything of the story. In return, Grant treated the journalist as though he were a member of the commander's official staff and rescinded the requirement for Cadwallader to submit his dispatches to a military censor prior to forwarding them on to his editors.

The *Herald* correspondent was very visible at Appomattox. Alone among the newspapermen who hovered around the surrender ceremonies, Cadwallader's dispatches were transmitted immediately to his New York office.

Kentucky-born Robert Anderson may have been assigned to command in Charleston Harbor because he once owned slaves and was the husband of a Georgia girl. Foes of U.S. Secretary of War John B. Floyd publicly charged that this was the case when Anderson's 1860 appointment was made public.

Regardless of what motives lay behind Floyd's decision, the southern-born professional soldier elevated duty above sectional loyalty. Moving his force into powerful but never-used Fort Sumter, he was a primary character in the drama that led to the outbreak of war.

After spending nearly three days on the receiving end of an artillery duel, Major Anderson was promoted to the rank of a Federal brigadier general. He was the only officer to jump two grades in rank immediately after surrendering his post.

English political leaders made only perfunctory attempts to hide their disdain when Charles Francis Adams Sr. reached London. He presented his credentials, was duly recognized as the U.S. minister to Great Britain, and tried to ignore the snubs.

Boston-born Adams, courtly in appearance and manners, soon made a friend. He was just the sort of person Prince Albert of Saxe-Coburg-Gotha enjoyed, so he spent considerable time with him.

Largely through the influence of Queen Victoria's consort, the American succeeded in his primary mission. Despite widespread sympathy for the Confederacy, he managed to prevent Parliament from recognizing the South as an independent nation. This, in turn, thwarted Secessionists who had planned to form military alliances with European nations at odds with the United States.

Adams also managed to put an end to British sales of warships to Confederates. Often overlooked today, his influence upon the outcome of the American conflict was second only to that of Lincoln. It was his patrician heritage, however, that made the minister unique. Among the sons of U.S. presidents, only Charles Francis Adams—son of John Quincy Adams and grandson of John Adams—played a prominent role in the Civil War.

Nathan Bedford Forrest grew up without a trace of formal schooling. In much the same fashion as Lincoln, but to a far less degree, he managed to educate himself. To keep the records needed by a livestock dealer, sixteen-year-old Forrest had to learn mathematics as well as how to read and write.

Forrest made enough money from cattle to support his family and soon had enough capital to enter the slave trade. Purchases of land in increasingly larger tracts enabled him to become a cotton planter of significance. As a result, Nathan B. Forrest accumulated assets of at least $1 million, a very large amount for that time. When he enlisted in the Seventh Tennessee Cavalry, he may have been the Confederacy's only millionaire private.

Soon he raised a cavalry battalion of his own and was rewarded by promotion to lieutenant colonel. Sometimes engaged in pitched battles but more often leading raids, the self-taught cavalry leader did not surrender until he learned that Lee had capitulated at Appomattox. In postwar years he was a railroad president and was a founder of the original Ku Klux Klan, which he left when he found the Klan's methods too brutal for his tastes.

Wealthy beyond the dreams of most southerners, Forrest occupies a Civil War niche that belongs to him alone. No other man who fought in either gray or blue enlisted as a private and surrendered as a lieutenant general.

Part Four

The Money Trail

Maj. Gen. William Tecumseh Sherman's terse "War is all hell" summation of the Civil War was neither overstatement nor hyperbole. A divided nation had exhausted almost every resource in the struggle that concerned manpower, industry, and inspiration.

Love of the Union was an ingredient that may have been as potent as sectional pride. Fierce resentment of directives from Washington was another essential contributor to the mix that exploded at Fort Sumter. These factors and many more combined to make the Civil War not only possible but inevitable. In looking at it from the perspective of several generations, we tend to emphasize such virtues as courage, self-sacrifice, obedience to orders, inventive ingenuity, and readiness to die in defense of home and region.

An essential ingredient, often overlooked, was money. Money played so many roles, some of them unobtrusive, that without it there would have been no war. It was the grease that made the wheels of the Federal and Confederate war machines move more or less smoothly.

The amount of money expended from 1861 to 1865 is startling. This is magnified when the relative value of a dollar then and now is taken into account. By the most conservative estimate, in the last decade of the twentieth century the purchasing power of $1 very roughly corresponds to 2½¢ or 3¢ during the Civil War. Thus without taking into account wartime inflation or the depreciation of Confederate currency, a single wartime dollar bought the equivalent of $33 to $40 today.

Salmon P. Chase was Lincoln's secretary of the treasury and the man responsible for paying the war bills. [HARPER'S HISTORY OF THE CIVIL WAR]

CHAPTER

13

Big Tickets to Small Change

U.S. animals, wagons, tools, clothing, ordnance, and commissary stores surrendered to Confederates in Texas before the surrender of Fort Sumter were valued at $1,209,500. U.S. Brig. Gen. David E. Twiggs, sometimes known as "Old Davy," surrendered all federal property without firing a shot. An itemized evaluation shows that the lost matériel included 1,800 mules and 950 horses whose combined value was $232,500.

During the fiscal year that ended on July 1, 1862, money expended for the Union military effort averaged $1,300,000 per day. During the same period, annual Federal expenditures for pensions and for Indians totaled only $3,102,985.50.

Philip Kearny was by no means the wealthiest of military leaders. Yet he may have been the man who pocketed the largest amount of cash without working for it. When his grandfather died in 1836, the future U.S. brigadier inherited substantially more than $1,000,000—almost enough to pay for one day of the war during its first year.

Samuel Colt patented the first of many revolvers in 1836, but his manufacturing company floundered, then failed. Revived by the Mexican War, in 1861 and 1862 his Patent Arms Manufacturing Company sold 107,000 .44-caliber weapons to the U.S. War Department. These sales alone netted $1,375,000 for the inventor-manufacturer.

According to the *Philadelphia Press,* Southern pride reached an apex of sorts late in 1861. During three months, the Northern journal reported, the seceded states contributed $1,515,898 to the Confederate armies.

During the fiscal year that ended on June 20, 1862, the U.S. government received $1,795,331.78 from "direct taxes" imposed upon the states. Since levies were made upon seceded states that refused to pay, their arrears created an enormous problem for them during the early months of Reconstruction.

Convinced that numerous Secessionists were still on the Federal payroll, Lincoln didn't trust conventional procedures. Although military supplies were desperately needed, he feared that the money would not be used properly.

As a result, the president took unprecedented action. He drew a voucher upon the U.S. Treasury in the sum of $2 million. Then he turned the cash over to John A. Dix, George Opdyke, and Richard M. Blatchford. No security, or bond, was required of these three civilians who were told to buy as many essentials for the war effort as they could.

Responding to the ensuing criticism, the president sent a special message to Congress on May 27, 1862. In it he insisted: "I believe that by this and similar measures taken in that crisis, some of which were without any authority of law, the Government was saved from overthrow. I am not aware that a dollar of the public funds thus confided without authority of law, to unofficial persons, was either lost or wasted."

Before New Orleans fell into Federal hands in April 1862, local leaders saw that surrender was near. Officers of major banks, a contemporary report claimed, packed $2 million in gold and currency into nine barrels labeled as beef. This consignment was then shipped up the Red River by commercial steamer.

In August 1863 the steamer *Ruth* had a special cargo aboard in the form of U.S. funds amounting to $2.5 million. When the vessel caught fire on the Mississippi River, flames raced through it so rapidly that not a single dollar was saved.

A congressional committee reported in 1863 that the cost of the war to the Federal government had reached $2.5 million a day.

Draft riots occurred throughout the North but were most violent in New York City. [NEW YORK PUBLIC LIBRARY]

After draft riots rocked New York City in July 1863, Mayor George Opdyke received from the city council a new ordinance authorizing payment of "commutation," or reparation, to persons whose property had been damaged. Eventually vetoed by the chief executive of the nation's largest city, the $2.5 million involved was estimated to be enough "to cover a substantial part of the losses occasioned by public resistance to military conscription."

During the conflict, expenditures for the U.S. Military Telegraph Service amounted to $2,655,500. Until 1863, the cost of providing and using the system was only $22,000 per month. It increased to $38,500 per month during that year, and in 1864 soared to $93,500 per month.

Published twenty-five years after the war's end, *War of the Rebellion—Official Records of the Union and Confederate Armies* ran to 128 volumes. The cost of the enterprise, completed in 1890 after having been inaugurated by U.S. Secretary of War Edwin M. Stanton, ran to $2,858,514.67.

In May 1862 Com. Andrew H. Foote received a gratifying report. According to it, until that date the cost of building and maintaining the flotilla of Federal gunboats on the Mississippi River was a bit under $3 million.

On August 13, 1863, Federal forces launched a raid into central Mississippi. Starting from LaGrange, Tennessee, cavalry and mounted infantry struck Oxford and Grenada. This foray produced one of many paths of destruction; although minor by comparison with others, it was estimated by the *Rebellion Record* to have destroyed Confederate property valued at not less than $3 million.

The cost of the war mounted more rapidly than did casualty figures. By 1865, military expenditures of the U.S. government reached a total just under $4 million a day.

Initially violently opposed by many military leaders, the U.S. Sanitary Commission received $4,813,750.64 from July 17, 1861, to July 1, 1865. Expenditures came to $4,530,774.92. Since it was impossible to keep records concerning the exact value of supplies sent to battlefields, hospitals, and camps, they were estimated at an even $15 million.

From 1861 to 1865 mills owned and operated by the DuPont family produced gunpowder for the Federal government valued at $6,861,922.

Two of the most active and successful Confederate vessels, the *Florida* and the *Alabama,* captured or destroyed ships and cargoes valued at $12,498,033.

Federal recruitment was comparatively haphazard until a Bureau for Enrollment and Conscription was organized on March 17, 1863. Brig. Gen. James B. Fry, serving as provost marshal general of the agency, reported that prior to the bureau's establishment, 1,356,593 men entered the Federal military establishment at an average cost of $34.01 per man, or a prebureau cost of $11,026,910. This amount greatly exceeded the $4,613,772 Fry and his subordinates spent in recruiting 1,120,621 men at an average cost of $9.84 per man.

At war's end, the United States demanded that Great Britain make reparation for ships and cargoes taken by Confederate raiders built in the United Kingdom. Eleven vessels were said to have inflicted damage amounting to $19,021,000.

If the report of the commissioners concerning British-rooted damage to U.S. shipping was accurate, the total was surprisingly close to that of the 1860 tax apportionment of all thirty-four states. From Alabama through Wisconsin, taxes claimed by the states amounted to $19,637,126.

Union paymasters reached the vicinity of Knoxville just as an artillery duel commenced. Fearful that any money they disbursed might fall into enemy hands, these officers "sat by the side of their twenty or thirty millions of dollars" until they were confident of a Federal victory.

Prior to the war, angry southerners were correct in charging that the chief source of revenue for the U.S. government was the Customs Service. Since industry was concentrated in the North, goods imported into the agricultural South accounted for the bulk of receipts for a twelve-month period reported as having been $49,056,897.62. During the same time the sale of public lands brought to federal coffers only $152,293.77.

Except in unusual circumstances, soldiers in blue were expected to be paid at ninety-day intervals. During periods of continuous fighting, it often proved impossible to maintain this schedule. As a result, newspapers reported late in January 1863 that "paymasters left Washington this week to deliver part of the $60 million in overdue pay to Union soldiers."

Data concerning the value of industrial production in the South during the war were not preserved. Within the Union, shoes were used in such immense quantities that their manufactured value was calculated to have been $91.9 million.

Surprisingly, textiles manufactured in the North during the war years surpassed shoes by only a small margin. With uniforms included, their value was just $115.6 million.

Although there was comparatively little fighting on the seas during 1865, expenditures for the U.S. Navy that year amounted to $123 million.

Food required an even bigger outlay than did shoes. During the fiscal year 1863–64, the Federal government appropriated $140 million to feed the army.

During the peak year of 1862, an estimated six thousand blockade-runners defied the U.S. Navy to enter and leave Confederate ports. The value of the goods brought to the seceded states from England and Europe during the entire conflict has been estimated at around $200 million.

Top officials of the U.S. Navy were pleased when final tabulations of wartime expenditures were made. According to them, warships and their batteries and crews accounted for only 9.3 percent of the total cost of the war to the Federal government. If that figure is correct, the Union expended only $314 million for enterprises that included the blockade, which is considered to have been one of its most successful efforts.

To boost enlistment in Federal armed forces, a system of bounties was developed very early. Men who volunteered to serve for ninety days in 1862 received $25 from Uncle Sam, while those who signed up for a year got twice as much. Rising throughout the conflict, the bounty paid to a five-year volunteer after March 1863 was $400.

Most states, many cities, and numerous villages paid additional bounties. Total cash handed out as bounty payments probably exceeded $750 million.

Jay Cook, only forty years old at the outbreak of the conflict, became the chief financial adviser to U.S. Secretary of the Treasury Salmon P. Chase. Soon he was made the sole agent for the sale of U.S. government bonds to both public and private investors.

During a single six-month period, Jay Cook and Company sold government paper whose face value exceeded $850 million.

Federal paymasters were required to keep meticulous records, usually in duplicate or triplicate. On October 31, 1865, their disbursements that had begun on July 12, 1861, were tabulated. During this period, officers and men of the U.S. Army received $1,029,239,000. New York City topped this figure. According to the *Journal of the Board of Aldermen*, the municipal government paid for equipping regiments with arms and ammunition and for relief of soldiers' families in the amount of $1,038,278,000.

Late in 1865, the directors of a principal railroad of the Confederacy issued a report on its wartime losses. The cost of the conflict to the Georgia Railroad and Banking Company was listed at $2,232,528.71.

All estimates of the value of slaves freed during and after the conflict are suspect. One yardstick is found in congressional records. At the insistence of the president, lawmakers offered to reimburse owners in the amount of $67,644,900 on condition that all slaves would be freed.

In 1860, according to *The Statistical History of the United States*, there were 3,953,760 slaves in the country. If a "reasonable" figure of $400 per slave is used to factor the total cost of the population, then that figure would be around $1.6 billion.

In 1865 the national public debt was about $75.01 per person, or a total of $2,677,929,000. In 1861, when Maj. Robert Anderson moved his command to Fort Sumter from Fort Moultrie, a levy of $2.06 per person would have wiped out the federal debt of $64,844,000.

The total cost of the war in which an estimated 4,178,000 men fought cannot be calculated with accuracy. Federal records, considered to be reasonably accurate and complete, indicate that the outlay of the Union reached at least $3.02 billion. Since property losses were much greater in the South than in the North, the conflict may have cost the Confederates $4 billion.

That $7 billion total is almost equal to the appraised value of all real and personal property in every state in 1850. In terms of the purchasing power of the 1995 dollar, the Civil War cost $231 billion to $280 billion.

During one of the times when U.S. Maj. Gen. William Tecumseh Sherman had Memphis under his control, an enterprising merchant brought in two boxcars filled with merchandise but marked as "Relief Association." When Sherman discovered the ruse, he confiscated the shipment.

A Federal officer who witnessed the proceedings reported that the confiscated goods were sold within twenty-four hours, yielding $8,000 to the U.S. government.

When the patriotic citizens of New York's Oneida County wanted to aid the war effort, wealthy Charles Wheelock organized the Ninety-seventh New York Volunteers. Once he was elected colonel of the outfit, he assumed all responsibility for the dependents left by the soldiers. According to the *New York Tribune,* Wheelock parted with "upward of nine thousand dollars out of his own pocket towards the support of the families."

On May 21, 1863, a band of guerrillas rode into Pittsburg, Missouri. Soon they discovered that a local bank was a depository for state funds. Before sundown, they departed "carrying with them eleven thousand dollars belonging to the State."

In April 1864 a band of about a thousand men in blue marched down a bank of the Tennessee River toward Decatur, Alabama. Serving under the command of Brig. Gen. John W. Geary, they halted for the night at a hamlet near Bridgeport. When the soldiers entered the tiny town, they discovered and seized "mail and seventeen thousand dollars in Confederate money."

Many of the folk who lived in the mountains of western Virginia were more than ready to create a new state. Backed by Lincoln, they established West Virginia.

This movement, seldom recognized as a form of secession from the Old Dominion, couldn't operate without cash. Hence the dissidents seized $30,000 in Virginia funds to begin to implement their independence.

The money had been deposited in the Exchange Bank of Weston, where it was placed to the credit of the Western Lunatic Asylum. Civilian-soldiers who seized the cache "aroused the drowsy population by playing 'The Star-Spangled Banner' before demanding the cash."

Since a detail of men from the Seventh Ohio Infantry had assisted the rebellious West Virginians, they were rewarded by the man who called himself governor of the new state. Francis H. Pierpont, soon to be recognized in Washington as governor, gave the soldiers 10 percent of the money they helped to seize. "Thus was the Restored Government organized," Boyd B. Stutler wrote many years later, "the most unusual state that ever belonged to the Union."

Late in September 1860, a Federal provost marshal issued a proclamation in Saint Louis to announce that $33,000 belonging to Cherokees had been "confiscated to the use and benefit of the United States."

The money involved represented a portion of the annual annuity promised to the Cherokees at the time of their removal from Georgia to Oklahoma.

According to the *New York Herald* of August 18, 1860, an unidentified band of U.S. troops staged a successful raid at Sainte Genevieve, Missouri. Some readers of the eastern newspaper were surprised to learn that $58,000 was seized.

R. C. Gridley of Nevada unsuccessfully solicited gifts for the U.S. Sanitary Commission, having specified to his friends and neighbors that he wanted them to be generous.

Refusing to be foiled in his effort to raise money for the organization of volunteers, Gridley tried a novel scheme. He put a twenty-pound sack of flour into a benefit auction. The gift changed hands several times, each seller following his example of contributing the purchase money. Gridley's flour eventually boosted the resources of the Sanitary Commission by $3,500 a pound, for a total gift to the agency of $70,000.

When North Carolina attorney Jacob Thompson was the chief Confederate agent in Canada, he was not required to give a detailed accounting of money sent to him. After the war, however, Judah P. Benjamin, one-time Confederate secretary of the treasury, became suspicious and hinted that he would request an audit of Thompson's books. This prompted the Tarheel to turn over to former Confederates about $60,000.

After Benjamin ceased to ask questions, Thompson took the remaining $113,000 from his accounts and spent the next few years living luxuriously in Europe.

Judah P. Benjamin served for a time as Confederate secretary of the treasury. [BATTLES AND LEADERS]

Confederate Maj. James Nocquet had been selected to safeguard funds that were designated for a number of military construction projects. Shortly after the November 25, 1863, battle of Missionary Ridge, he was seen making his way toward Federal lines. His progress was somewhat slow, as he carried with him an estimated $150,000 that aides of Gen. Braxton Bragg had planned to spend on roads and defensive works.

Near Kearneysville in what had become West Virginia, Confederate raider John S. Mosby directed his men to tear up a section of railroad track. Soon a passenger train of the Baltimore and Ohio Railroad hit the trap at full speed.

The waiting Confederates headed straight toward a baggage car believed to be transporting two U.S. Army paymasters. When they pried open the door of the car, it took the bandits in uniform only a few minutes to scoop up $173,000 before they burned the train.

Famous—or infamous—as the Greenback Raid, this exploit took place in a gorge on October 13, 1864. The jubilant Southerners returned to their base to the strains of music produced by two fiddlers who knew only one tune, "Malbrook Has Gone to the Wars."

Saint Albans, Vermont, was the site of the northernmost Confederate raid of the war. On October 19, 1864, Lt. Bennet H. Young led a band of about twenty-five volunteers into the town that lay only fifteen miles south of the Canadian border.

Three banks were robbed, yielding a total of $201,522. Within days more than one-third of the stolen money was recovered.

U.S. Maj. Gen. Benjamin F. Butler learned that some of the banks of New Orleans held considerable sums. Citing a congressional act of July 17, 1862, as his authority, he seized Confederate funds believed to be in excess of $250,000.

On March 14, 1861, members of the provisional Confederate Congress adopted a resolution of thanks directed to "the convention of the State of Louisiana." It lauded "the patriotic liberality" of lawmakers whose metropolis was New Orleans.

Earlier, Confederates of the port city had seized from U.S. authorities a "bullion fund" in the amount of $389,267.46. It was soon turned over to the Confederate government by A. J. Guirot of the Louisiana State Depository. At Montgomery, delighted Secessionists soon learned that $147,519.66 more would come their way. This sum represented U.S. customs collections at New Orleans after January 31 of the year in which war broke out.

Confederates were not the only ones to seize cash in New Orleans. As military governor of the city, Union General Butler concluded that funds held by the Dutch consul had been sent for safekeeping by Southerners who planned to purchase war supplies.

Disregarding diplomatic immunity, he ordered Federal troops to raid the consulate, taking from it $800,000.

South Carolina led the way in seizing Federal installations within the borders of seceded states. F. C. Humphreys, storekeeper of military supplies, made no attempt to resist when armed men surrounded his building on December 30, 1860.

The value of the arsenal, which occupied the whole of a city block, is unknown. In addition, Secessionists seized weapons that ranged in size from pistols to cannon. The value of more than

Weapons seized from the U.S. Arsenal at Charleston were soon put to use by South Carolina troops. [PICTORIAL HISTORY OF THE CONFEDERACY]

twenty-two thousand pieces of ordnance acquired that day by the Palmetto State was conservatively estimated to be "well in excess of $350,000."

Once it was certain that an armed conflict would take place, Southern leaders made it known that they were in desperate need of cash. As a result, the state of Alabama made a loan of $500,000 to the central government then established in Montgomery. Had this money not been available, Confederate troops would have been unable to meet the Federal invaders of Virginia soil at Manassas.

Confederate units led by Maj. Gen. J. E. B. Stuart descended upon Federal headquarters on August 22, 1863. As Union Maj. Gen. John Pope had been comfortably established at Catlett's Station for some time, several money chests were stored there.

Members of Stuart's Ninth Virginia Cavalry made off with Pope's personal belongings, some of his horses, and his dispatch book. In addition, they took the contents of the Federal money chests, approximately $520,000.

Commanders of warships that made up Federal blockading squadrons had orders to seize cotton whenever possible. So much of it accumulated that U.S. Secretary of the Treasury Salmon P. Chase decided it was time to do something with it.

Thus Hiram Barney, a Federal cotton agent in New York, was authorized to sell everything in the Federal warehouses. In February 1863 he reported that he had sold 3,325 bales of cotton. Additional cotton that had not been ginned was estimated at 1,779 bales. Net proceeds to the Federal government amounted to $696,562.

An ardently pro-Confederate, former governor Sterling Price of Missouri took command of state troops in 1860. He captured Lexington, Missouri, in September 1861 and triumphantly reported having found $900,000 that Federals had earlier taken from banks in the state.

In addition to the cash, Price seized commissary stores whose estimated value was $100,000. Reporting to Gov. Claiborne F. Jackson, he said this raid netted well over $1 million since he seized "over 3,000 stand of infantry arms and about 750 horses."

En route to Falmouth, England, the commercial vessel *B. F. Hoxie* carried papers showing that her cargo included a quantity of expensive logwood. She was seized by a privateer in June 1863 at a point described as "latitude twelve degrees north, longitude thirty degrees."

When men from the crew of the raider *Florida* broke open the hold of the captured vessel, they found that in addition to wood she carried silver bars and thirty tons of silver ore. The bars were appraised at $500,000, and the ore was estimated to be worth about the same.

Gov. Oliver P. Morton of Indiana personally led recruitment campaigns that sent regiment after regiment into Federal service. Since the state included thousands of Democrats who opposed the war, legislators balked at providing the funds needed for Morton's troops.

An impasse was reached when it became evident that the Hoosier chief executive had to choose between only two alternatives. He could disband many of his regiments or he could find a way to circumvent the state legislature. Morton therefore

Federal forces seized huge quantities of cotton and sold it at auction.
[GEORGIA HISTORICAL SOCIETY]

borrowed more than $1 million to spend on pay, uniforms, muskets, and artillery.

Michigan responded eagerly when Lincoln issued his first call for volunteers. Historically, its lawmakers had provided an annual appropriation of only $3,000 for the twenty-eight militia companies of the state.

On May 7, 1862, with civil war a certainty, the legislature hurriedly passed a magnanimous fiscal act. Under its terms, the state that earlier begrudged $3,000 a year for military purposes authorized the governor to raise ten regiments and float a loan of $1 million to arm and equip them.

On September 3, 1861, Unionist readers of the *National Intelligencer* were gratified by a detailed report concerning the activities of a federal official described as the "surveyor of the port of New York." During the five months immediately following the surrender of Fort Sumter, this official had seized eight ships, seven barks, and ten other vessels "owned wholly or in part by rebels." The value of the twenty-five privately owned ships confiscated in the port of New York was reported to be more than $2 million.

On September 15, 1863, Union Rear Adm. David D. Porter sent a special report to Washington describing some minor military actions. One of these occurred near Bolivar, Tennessee, where three Confederate paymasters had been captured. Escorted by thirty-five men, the money carriers had been headed toward Little Rock with $2.5 million. Although the entire sum was captured, it did not affect U.S. balance sheets since men in gray were to be paid in Confederate currency.

After 1861 British investors owned most blockade-runners. A postwar summary indicated that "total loss to owners who ventured in the business was in the neighborhood of $30 million."

Under a series of congressional acts, the U.S. Treasury was authorized to issue interest-bearing notes during the 1850s. On January 1, 1861, Federal obligations incurred through distribution of these notes amounted to $17,387,011.64.

When Lincoln issued the call for volunteers, fiscal authorities switched from notes to bonds. More than two weeks before the first battle of Manassas, a "loan bill" passed the U.S. House of Representatives. When five issues of bonds authorized before the first major battle had been sold, the U.S. national debt increased by $250 million.

Soon after Appomattox, the ladies of Montgomery, Alabama, formed a Memorial Association. Twenty-five years later, the body passed a resolution authorizing erection on Capitol Hill of a monument to the state's Confederate dead. The cost, when completed, was not to exceed $45,000.

To help raise the money, the ladies "gave an entertainment for the great monument, in which all alike are interested." This fundraising event brought to the Memorial Association a net profit of $143.85. Presumably their other efforts met with greater success since the monument is there today.

Soldiers in gray who were stationed in San Antonio at war's end knew that the city was a depository for Confederate silver. They raided the government vault, divided the silver among themselves, and each man became richer by $160.

When the USS *San Jacinto* was wrecked in 1865, what was left of the vessel was sold. An auction resulted in a gain for the U.S. Treasury of $224.61.

After the U.S. government resorted to enforced conscription for military service, a man in any Northern state could hire a substitute. During 1863 in nearly every part of the Union a fellow who agreed to go to the battlefield in place of a draftee pocketed at least $300.

Throughout the Cotton Belt, desperate need for gunboats induced women to hold fairs to raise money. At Tuskegee, Alabama, a different approach was tried in early 1862. Five ladies used columns of the *Advertiser and Register* to reach the general public. The newspaper reported that: "The patriotic ladies of Tuskegee desire to be represented in the enterprise that has for its object the protection of their dearest rights. For this purpose they have canvassed the community, and have secured cash subscriptions to the amount of $303.95, together with a donation of three bales of cotton."

At Pensacola, Confederates met in hand-to-hand combat with Federal soldiers during the fall of 1861. A letter written from the scene of the action reported, "We killed about one hundred of them, and lost heavily in killed and wounded on our side, but I do not know the exact number."

Pockets of the Federal dead were quickly emptied, the letter-writer added. Loot included "coats, hats, caps, swords, and a fine pair of navy pistols." Even better, in the opinion of the writer, "One of our men got three hundred and forty dollars in cash."

While bank employees in Saint Albans, Vermont, were being held at gunpoint by Confederate raiders, a local merchant came to pay off a note. Sam Breck was quickly spotted as carrying cash in his right hand. Hence the soldiers pushed him into a backroom of the bank, relieved him of the cash, and added $393 to their take.

The adjutant general of the U.S. Army, Samuel Cooper, became a tormented man before the outbreak of war. Born and reared in New Jersey, he graduated from West Point in 1815 and soon married a Virginia belle. With war looming, he decided in early March 1861 to join the Secessionists.

Cooper became a brigadier on March 16 and was the moving force behind the organization of the Confederate army. Soon he received a commission making him a full general, ranking from May 16. As the senior general officer of forces in gray, Cooper did more than anyone except Davis and Lee to keep the Confederacy alive.

By 1870 he was a "dirt poor farmer" in Alexandria, Virginia, who was barely able to subsist. Vividly conscious of Cooper's monumental labor for the Lost Cause, Lee solicited contributions from veterans.

Former Confederates who responded to the appeal from the one-time commander of the Army of Northern Virginia sent him $300. With a personal gift from Lee added, "the Samuel Cooper Relief Fund" reached a total of $400.

Pennsylvania-born mechanic Samuel Ruth took a course opposite to that of Cooper. When the war began, he had lived in Virginia for many years and was regarded by neighbors and fellow workers as a true-blue supporter of the Confederacy. By this time he had become superintendent of transportation for an all-important railroad that ran from Richmond to the Potomac River by way of Fredericksburg.

Ruth successfully hid his strong Unionist sentiments for months, then secretly made contact with Federal military leaders. For at least two years, he served as a spy who fed to Washington vital information about railroad movements.

After the surrender at Appomattox, he dropped the pretense, admitted what he had done, and applied for compensation. Early requests from Ruth seem to have been ignored, but his claim for having rendered services worth $40,000 was eventually processed. From the capital, the spy whose life was daily laid on the line for two years received a check for $500.

CHAPTER

14

Payday Some Day

A widely circulated report has it that South Carolina was the only state that did not raise a single regiment for Federal service. Despite its prevalence, the account is not correct. From January to July 1863, four regiments of South Carolina infantry were raised to fight Confederates. Both the First and the Second South Carolina Infantry (African Descent) saw limited combat service.

Organized at Hilton Head in June, the Third South Carolina Infantry (African Descent) spent more than seven months there on post duty. Moving to Jacksonville, Florida, in February 1864, during March it became the Twenty-first U.S. Colored Troops.

Sgt. William Walker of Company A was disgruntled when he learned that regulations called for men in blue to be paid only at ninety-day intervals. To make matters worse, no paymaster appeared after members of the Third South Carolina had drilled and drilled and drilled for that long period. Members of the regiment devised a song whose melodious refrain was simply, "P-a-a-y-day, some d-a-a-y!"

Col. Thomas W. Higginson, destined to gain fame and die with the Fifty-fourth Massachusetts Infantry, sympathized but could do nothing. In his diary he noted that the pay issue "impaired discipline, relaxed loyalty, and has begun to implant a feeling of sullen distrust" among black soldiers.

Walker, who was exempt from conscription, had volunteered and enrolled on April 24. By August he was so angry that he was charged with using threatening language when addressing an officer. Soon a court-martial was convened and the man who wanted only to be paid was put on trial. Convicted, he was reduced to the rank of private and sentenced "to be shot to death with musketry."

An unidentified soldier, believed to be a native of South Carolina. [CHICAGO HISTORICAL SOCIETY]

On February 29, 1864, Walker paid with his life for having waged a one-man fight to get the U.S. government to pay a just debt.

One man whose pay came from the U.S. government never complained that his money would arrive some day. It invariably came to Abraham Lincoln on schedule, at the rate of about $70 a day or $2,083 per month.

Lincoln's $25,000 per year was princely in comparison with all military and most civilian salaries. His wife, however, seems to have been a compulsive buyer, whose spending sprees packed the White House closets with shoes and garments that were never worn. Despite the idiosyncrasies of Mary Todd Lincoln, the frugal president had accumulated about $90,000 by the time he was felled by a bullet from John Wilkes Booth's derringer. After the president's death, unredeemed salary warrants worth $4,044.67 were found in his desk.

Mary Todd Lincoln had specific ideas about what was appropriate for the White House and the First Family regardless of the cost. [BRADY STUDIO, LIBRARY OF CONGRESS]

In 1862 Edwin M. Stanton of Ohio was approached about becoming U.S. secretary of war. When he learned that the position paid $8,000 annually his initial reaction was negative. "I can't afford to give up a thriving law practice for such a sum," he said.

After deciding to join Lincoln's cabinet, Stanton chose Peter H. Watson to be assistant secretary of war. For $3,000 a year and some prestige, Watson often worked more than one hundred hours a week.

Confederate Secretary of State Judah P. Benjamin was paid $6,000 a year in 1862. His chief clerk, L. Q. Washington, tried to make ends meet on $1,750 a year—in Confederate currency already depreciating rapidly.

When the provisional Confederate Congress was organized at Montgomery, Alabama, the elected representatives were given a per diem allowance of $8 a day. In 1861, many of them collected a total of about $450.

This situation changed rapidly, despite the fact that no member of the body had significant seniority. In April 1862 the *Richmond*

Whig berated Southern lawmakers for accepting "about five thousand four hundred dollars per annum from the public treasury." As a result, raged the newspaper, a man whose only risk came from harsh words received about $2,700 more for a year's service than did a colonel on the battlefield.

Neither editorials nor public opinion had any effect. Knowing that the collapse of the Confederacy was near and with their government deeply in debt, Confederate lawmakers boosted their own salaries to $16,500 per year.

Members of the Maryland legislature did not fare nearly so well as did Confederate congressmen. In 1861 they were paid $4 a day to try to keep the divided state out of war.

About the time of Lincoln's first inauguration, the Confederate provisional Congress tackled the difficult question of military structure and pay. It was comparatively easy to decide to authorize formation of one corps of engineers and another of artillery, plus six regiments of infantry and one of cavalry.

Starting at the top, lawmakers provided for the selection of four brigadiers, each to be paid $3,612 per year. A chief aide-de-camp, with the minimum rank of lieutenant, would start at $125 per month.

Some officers in other branches of Confederate service were initially paid more than infantry officers of the same rank. In 1861 an infantry colonel drew $195, while a colonel of artillery received $210 monthly. Pay of a major ranged from $150 in the infantry to $162 in the cavalry.

For their surgeon general, the Confederate lawmakers provided $3,000 per year "plus fuel and quarters." In the U.S. Army a surgeon with ten years of military experience was eligible to draw $200 per month, but one who had practiced for only nine years received $162 per month.

Commanders of an army in the field were allowed an extra $100 per month. Anticipating the possibility of a struggle much longer than was then foreseen in Washington, lawmakers assembled at Montgomery voted to give an extra $9 per month to every commissioned officer who reached the five-year service mark.

A sergeant or master workman of a Confederate engineer corps was eligible for pay at the rate of $34 per month, while corporals and overseers received $20. An infantry private was paid $11 per month plus clothing and one food ration per day.

Two years later, with merchants often refusing to accept Confederate currency at face value, the pay for men in gray was substantially the same. A general, regardless of grade, still received $301 monthly. Some disgusted privates grumbled that their commanders received $1 per month for the services they rendered, with the balance thrown in "to please them." By war's end, a full general in gray was due to receive Confederate currency in the amount of $328 per month.

Many officers' pay was supplemented by a formal scale regarding the number of horses allowed for their use. Assistant surgeons received two animals at government expense, and generals of all ranks were allowed four. Cavalrymen under the rank of first lieutenant were required to provide their own mounts.

Battlefield experience soon demonstrated the necessity or desirability of using persons not initially listed as military personnel. Hence by 1863 Confederate armies were paying hospital stewards $20 or $21 per month and a hospital matron received all of $6 per month. Chaplains, added as an afterthought, received $80 per month, according to *Regulations for the Army of the Confederate States.*

Although the Confederate Marine Corps was never large, it was elite. Lawmakers initially envisioned it as comprising not more than 621 men and commanded by a major. With authorized strength boosted to 1,000, this body finally included about 525 men.

By the time the corps attained that size, the pay of privates had been increased from $11 per month to $15. A marine corporal received an extra $2 per month, and a first sergeant's pay swelled to $24 monthly. Since a colonel's pay was considered to be generous, in the marine corps it remained at $195 per month.

Many a Confederate would have been amazed at the actions that led to William Walker's execution. Scores of units fought, marched, and fought again for more than a year before receiving a single dollar.

Men in blue sometimes fared no better. Pvt. Alfred S. Roe of the Ninth New York Heavy Artillery never forgot nor forgave. Long after the war ended, he lamented, "I never saw any of Uncle Sam's wages between January '64 and March '65."

Volunteers rushed to form Anderson's Cavalry (later the Fifteenth Pennsylvania) at Carlisle, Pennsylvania, in November

John C. Frémont was the first explorer to see spectacular formations along the Columbia River. [AUTHOR'S COLLECTION]

1861. This high-profile unit was formed to provide an escort and a headquarters guard for Brig. Gen. Robert Anderson of Fort Sumter fame. Now a brigadier in Kentucky, Anderson was delighted to receive volunteers from the Keystone State. These Federals were paid nothing until December 1862, more than thirteen months after having first mounted their horses and flourished their sabers.

Theory—and regulations—called for Federal units to be mustered for pay at sixty-day intervals. Paymasters were supposed to be on hand the last day of February, April, June, August, and October. Perhaps as a sort of year end or Christmas bonus, the final payday of a calendar year was often scheduled for December 5. Many factors operated to prevent timely payments, however.

Union Maj. Gen. John C. Frémont didn't like the idea of asking men to fight without pay. After having made repeated futile requests to the War Department, he dispatched an urgent letter to Lincoln on July 30, 1861. In it, the man who had won civilian fame as "the Pathfinder" said that a U.S. depository in Saint Louis held "$300,000 entirely unappropriated."

Frémont had asked the official in charge to release $100,000 to the paymaster of the Western Department but was curtly refused. Reporting to the president, the man who in 1856 had been the first Republican candidate for the White House announced: "This morning I will order the Treasurer [in Saint Louis] to deliver the money in his possession, and will send a force to take the money, and will direct such payments as the exigency requires. I will hazard everything for the defense of the department you have confided to me, and I trust to you for support." If Lincoln acknowledged this imperious demand that soldiers be paid, his reply has vanished; it does not appear in his *Collected Works*.

Frémont's plan to seize and dispense these funds may have failed. In December, editors of the *Missouri Democrat* berated the War Department because members of the Twenty-seventh Missouri Infantry still had received no pay.

Bureaucrats of the War Department devised an ingenious scheme to juggle payments in favor of the U.S. Treasury. Having failed to smash the Army of Tennessee, U.S. Maj. Gen. William T. Sherman decided to capture Atlanta.

Sherman fired off a series of telegrams to the paymaster general in Washington, first requesting and then demanding that his troops be "mostly paid in checks on New York." On September 30, 1864, the general received a telegram from Maj. Gen. Henry W. Halleck that outlined a system devised for deferring payday.

Halleck, the U.S. chief of staff, informed Sherman that half of what was owed to Union soldiers was to be paid in the form of interest-bearing treasury notes or bonds. Such a remittance, he pointed out, "not being a legal tender by law, cannot be deposited and checked against." This meant that although soldiers who had followed Sherman from Chattanooga to Atlanta were paid in full legally, they could not use the money for weeks or months.

Women of the U.S. Sanitary Commission, no longer willing to see soldiers go penniless for months, established a "back-pay agency." Civilian volunteers took the soldiers' papers, ensured that they were in proper order, and learned how to knock on the right doors in Washington. A single branch of this agency sometimes received $20,000 from the capital in a single day.

Gov. John A. Andrew of Massachusetts was an ardent supporter of the war from start to finish. [BATTLES AND LEADERS]

Gov. John A. Andrew of Massachusetts was frustrated with the notorious delays in the army's paying its soldiers. In early 1863 he proposed that the state legislature empower the state treasurer to borrow funds to make pay advances to the men of Massachusetts serving in the Union army whose pay from Washington was late. The measure was approved. At the time, the pay for the First Massachusetts Cavalry was more than $200,000 in arrears.

At first, Lincoln was successful in opposing prisoner exchanges. Since he argued that no state had seceded, an exchange of prisoners would seem to elevate the Confederacy to the level of nationhood.

Practical considerations eventually forced him to abandon this point of view. Once the distinction was made, Federal authorities took action that granted prisoners of war the same pay they would have received if they had been on normal duty.

When misconceptions about the conflict began to clear and the country realized that the war would be a much longer affair than many had at first expected, lawmakers on both sides began to adjust the pay of soldiers. The pay of Union privates jumped from $11 to $13 per month in 1861 and eventually reached a peak of $16. Meanwhile, a private in gray saw his pay raised from $11 to $18 per month. At the time this increase took effect, in much of the Confederacy a pair of shoes cost $125 and coffee was hard to find at $12 a pound.

Some Native Americans who volunteered to fight in gray fared even worse than their Anglo counterparts. When Confederate Brig. Gen. Albert Pike authorized the raising of regiments during the fall of 1860, Creeks, Choctaws, and Cherokees responded with considerable enthusiasm. Their zeal for the Confederate cause, however, began to evaporate when they found that neither arms nor pay had been arranged for them. A disgusted officer later acknowledged that "with the exception of a partial supply for the Choctaw regiment, no tents, clothing, or camp and garrison equippage was furnished to any of them."

Federal officers were initially paid much less than their Southern counterparts. A brigadier received $124 per month and a major general was paid $220 monthly. Cash designated for colonels ranged from $95 to $110, depending upon the branch of service in which a man fought.

Pay differential for majors was $10 monthly, from $70 (infantry and artillery) to $80 (cavalry, ordnance, and engineers). Many a captain yearned to move from the infantry into the cavalry in order to boost his monthly pay from $60 to $70.

Unlike enlisted men, Federal officers were not issued rations in addition to cash. This often forced a man wearing stars on his shoulders to send out a servant or two to forage for him. This situation fostered widespread looting from civilians, regardless of their loyalty or lack of it.

After a Union officer pocketed $600 during a calendar year, the balance of his salary was subject to what Washington called "a special duty" of 3 percent. This highly effective device constituted the prototype of today's income tax withholding from wages and salaries.

Originally designated at ninety days, terms of enlistment in Federal forces were frequently and rapidly extended. By the time Grant closed the jaws of his military trap upon Lee, five-year volunteers were being enrolled.

A recruit who signed up for a sixty-month hitch was promised—but did not always get—clothing in addition to cash. Regulations called for such a person to receive during his five-year hitch the following equipment: two blankets, thirteen pairs of trousers, eight coats, fifteen flannel shirts, eleven pairs of drawers, twenty pairs of stockings, five hats, twelve caps, and, at three-month intervals, one pair of booties). In 1863, the *Revised Regulations for the Army of the United States* stipulated that "mounted men may receive one pair of boots and two pairs of bootees instead of four pairs of bootees."

In addition to having preferential treatment for their feet, Union cavalrymen who provided their own mounts and gear were paid for them during much of the conflict. An initial allowance of 50¢ per day for this purpose was quickly reduced to 40¢. Eventually having accumulated enough of its own horses to meet the need, the War Department dropped this special allowance.

Privates on both sides were promised one ration per day in addition to cash. Within Federal forces, any soldier of that rank could use as much as $42 worth of clothing in twelve months as a supplement to his pay. If he exceeded the annual limit, the cost of extra clothing was deducted by a paymaster.

Anyone who managed to spend a year on active duty without using his full clothing allowance was supposed to receive the difference in cash. Thus one of the typical activities following a battle was the systematic stripping of clothing from the dead.

After the Federal disaster at Manassas, a military nurse—almost always male—was paid at the rate of 40¢ per day plus one food ration.

Under the terms of a congressional act of July 17, 1862, Lincoln was authorized to employ African Americans "for the suppression of this rebellion." He was given a free hand to establish a system of organization with which to use them, but the act made no provision for their compensation.

William Whiting, solicitor of the War Department, handed down a ruling on April 25, 1863, stating that "persons of African descent who should be employed under the law should received $10 per month and one ration each per day, of which $3 might be paid in clothing." For practical purposes, this established the pay of a black volunteer at a trifle over half that drawn by a white comrade.

Racial tensions in the North mounted when a few free African Americans discovered that if they volunteered they would not receive the same bounties promised to whites. So serious was this matter that a congressional committee made a study, resulting in a special report about "Colored men and their relation to the military service."

The ambiguous language of the report complicated matters even more. With Federal draft laws in effect, the U.S. solicitor general was requested to look into the question of racially mixed substitutes. The opinion stated: "In compliance with special instructions from the President, an order was issued on the 20th of July, 1863, directing that men of African descent should only be accepted as substitutes for each other."

Thus Northerners could not avoid service in the Union army by hiring free blacks to fight for them. In many cities, African Americans would have accepted $200 gladly (two-thirds of the going rate) to serve as a substitute for a draftee.

Although still on the books, this provision was not being enforced in 1865. By that time, African-American soldiers were paid at the same rate as whites.

Pay for maritime service was generally higher than for service on land. A Confederate admiral drew $6,000 per year, and when commanding a squadron a captain was listed at $5,000. For other sea duty, a captain's pay dropped $800 per year. Yet while on leave or awaiting orders, such an officer drew $250 per month.

With five years' experience (usually most of it in the U.S. Navy), a Confederate commander on sea duty drew $2,825 per year. While awaiting assignment or on leave, such an officer received only $187.50 per month.

By January 1, 1863, *The Register of the Navy of the United States* reported that Federal naval officers had received significant raises in pay. At sea a commander drew $2,800 yearly, while a captain was paid $3,500. When a man moved from the rank of captain to commodore, his sea duty pay jumped $500 yearly.

For the newly created rank of rear admiral, the U.S. Navy Department provided $5,000 during sea duty. A rear admiral took a 20 percent cut in pay when he was assigned to shore duty, and other wearers of naval brass faced approximately the same differential.

Men of the Second Louisiana Regiment stormed Port Hudson's defenses on May 27, 1863. [LESLIE'S HISTORY OF THE CIVIL WAR]

For reasons never fully explained, the commanding officer of a warship whose pay was only $1,500 annually was also allowed one food ration per year without charge. Should such an officer take on the chores of paymaster, he drew an extra $200 a year.

A Federal surgeon on duty at sea drew $2,200 a year for five years, but this rose to $3,000 annually after twenty years of service. A chief engineer was paid at the rate of $150 per month for five years, but after fifteen years was boosted to $216.66. A naval gunner started at $1,000 per year and after twelve years reached a peak of $1,450.

Two sets of persons were at the bottom of the inverted pyramid that made up the pay scale of the U.S. Navy. A powder monkey, or "water boy," received $10 a month plus rations. Since this position called for sailors of a small, short stature, some of these youngsters had been recruited at nine years of age.

Once a shooting war got under way, these juveniles had competition for the position from older and larger African Americans. In

September 1861, U.S. Secretary of the Navy Gideon Welles released a directive, stipulating that "persons of color, commonly known as contrabands, may be enlisted as 'boys' at $10 per month and one ration per diem."

Civilian pay varied wildly, with geographical location and skills being major variables. Andrew Carnegie started as a bobbin boy in a Pennsylvania cotton mill and was paid $1.20 for a workweek of seventy-two or more hours.

Working in the sprawling Washington arsenal, a boy of twelve to sixteen years of age was paid, not by the hour, but by the piece. It took most of them a full day to put together 650 cartridges. As the need for ammunition grew more critical, the pay rose from about 60¢ a day to 75¢. Much piecework was also done at the U.S. Patent Office. In 1861 a typical employee received 80¢ for the skilled and laborious job of sewing a book by hand.

With plans underway for establishing the Gettysburg National Cemetery, another big job had to be done piece-by-piece. Thousands of bodies were exhumed at an average rate of $1.69 each.

A man working as a civilian medical corpsman for Federal forces was likely to be paid $20.50 monthly. Both the remuneration and the risk compared favorably with those of Pennsylvania coal miners, some of whom were lucky to get $275 per year and others who received as little as 50¢ per day.

In many sections of North Carolina and Tennessee, poor whites were glad to work for $110 a year plus food and clothes. Along the northwestern frontier of the United States, pay was substantially higher. A dependable workman could command as much as $14 a month in cash.

In cities along the eastern seaboard, a laborer with few skills was often paid $20 per month. At Elmira, New York, a veteran gravedigger received twice that amount.

Pay scales were almost always lower in the South than they were in the North. In New Orleans early in 1861 boys were lucky to earn 50¢ a day, while adult women often were paid 75¢ and unskilled men drew $1 a day. Some skilled workers received as much as $9 for a six-day workweek.

Carpenters working on the CSS *Mississippi* in 1861 were ordered off the job because they had banded together and demanded the impossibly high wage of $4 a day.

With a large proportion of young men in uniform, contractors who furnished fuel for wood-burning locomotives boosted their workers' wages to $3 a day, occasionally paying even more than that.

Newspaper members of the Southern Associated Press found themselves in the same bind by 1863. Fees for weekly reports of three thousand to four thousand words jumped to $12.

Veteran reporters and artists for widely circulated eastern newspapers fared even better. From the large dailies, they customarily drew $25 a week plus expenses. Winslow Homer was a conspicuous exception to the general rule. His work was in such demand that he was paid $60 a page.

A future major general, James A. Garfield, served for four prewar years as president of Ohio's Hiram College. In addition to his

At the U.S. Patent Office, many workers received "piece work pay" rather than a weekly wage. [NATIONAL ARCHIVES]

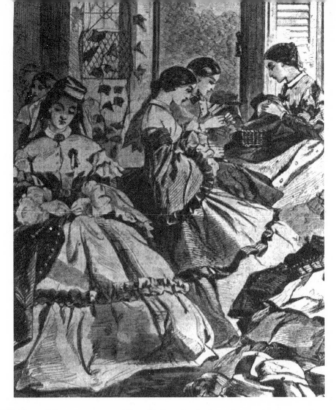

Artist Winslow Homer was paid well for depicting these women volunteers sewing havelocks for soldiers. [LIBRARY OF CONGRESS]

administrative duties, he lectured and taught penmanship. Garfield's salary was set by the college board of trustees at $80 per month.

When the famous Pony Express was launched in 1860, it was destined to survive only eighteen months, falling victim to rapidly expanding telegraph networks. A rider who went through Indian country from Saint Joseph, Missouri, to San Francisco in ten days was promised pay at the rate of $25 per month.

In New York, the 1862 annual report of the American Express Company reported that "two thousand men are in the regular employ of this company." The average salary was $600 per annum.

The Federal victory at Port Royal, South Carolina, made it easy for Northern entrepreneurs to come in and take possession of many large plantations. They soon discovered that they didn't know what to do with them. According to the *New York Tribune,* the new plantation owners promised to pay experienced overseers as much as $1,000 a year.

Salaries of the eight-man office working under the U.S. attorney general in 1861 ran to $20,500. Meanwhile, as confidential clerk to the commissioner of patents, Clara Barton was drawing $1,400 a year.

While the founder of the American Red Cross was working at the patent office, William Tecumseh Sherman took on the job of superintending the operation of the Saint Louis Car Company. This system of street transportation paid the future general $2,000 annually for his services.

Four years earlier another future general became chief engineer of the Illinois Central Railroad. In that capacity George B. McClellan was paid $3,000 a year for three years.

At war's end, P. G. T. Beauregard returned to his native New Orleans, financially ruined. After serving as president of a railroad, the renowned former Confederate general became superintendent of the state lottery. In this position, he was paid $30,000 annually—20 percent more than Lincoln's wartime salary.

15

For the Right Price

One of the least expensive things any military unit took to the battlefield was an eagle. At Eau Claire, Wisconsin, the regiment initially known as the Eau Claire Badgers wanted a mascot. For $2.50 they purchased a young eagle and called it Old Abe in honor of the president.

Union Adm. David D. Porter designed and built what was probably the least expensive craft of the war. He fastened two old lifeboats and a rotten flatboat together. Scrap canvas covered the three-hundred-foot contraption, upon which he mounted a set of "Quaker guns" made from logs. For fake smokestacks the Federal officer used a pair of pork barrels.

When placed where currents would carry it toward Confederate positions, the dummy ironclad created consternation when first spotted, but the Southerners soon saw that it posed no threat to them. It was not until much later that anyone outside of Porter's command knew that the cost of construction was calculated at $8.63.

In the North, pocket watches were prized by clerks, workmen, and sometimes by soldiers. The cost of such a timepiece climbed from $12 in 1861 to about $20 in 1863.

Before the start of hostilities, a target telescope could be purchased for about $20. The cost of less-expensive, mass-produced pieces ranged from $14 to $30.

When given his commission as a signal officer of the U.S. Army, Albert J. Myer compiled a list of essentials and their cost. A "complete set of day and night signal apparatus," he reported in July

Men using a signal apparatus sometimes placed them on short log towers.
[LIBRARY OF CONGRESS]

1860, could be purchased for $30. Before the end of the year, the cost of these instruments ranged between $44 and $60.

Early telegraph lines erected for Federal forces were built on contract. In the mountains of western Virginia, the bids averaged about $45 per mile. In Missouri, the same work cost about $100 per mile.

Fearful that persons on the U.S. government payroll couldn't be trusted, Lincoln assigned early purchases of military goods to civilians. No one knows what they paid for a soldier's uniform and equipment, exclusive of weapons. When the Quartermaster's Department began to buy in quantity, a soldier could be put into the field for $50 plus the cost of his musket or rifle.

When Confederate Lt. James H. Young of the Forty-second Georgia Infantry was killed at Chickasaw Bayou late in December 1862, most of his possessions were sold at auction in Atlanta. Some of the prices fetched were: $25 for his saddle and shotgun, $80 for fifteen hogs, $35 for his watch, $100 for a cow and calf, $27 for two jars of lard, and $150 for a buggy and harness.

Whether working at home or in improvised mills, each person processing cotton had to have a pair of cards, a tool consisting of pieces of fine wire set in thick leather and mounted on a piece of wood. Used to untangle fibers before spinning, the pair cost 40¢ at Savannah in 1861. By 1865 the same tool was worth $30 in northern Mississippi.

By March 1862 "moveable electric trains" were in wide use by Union commanders. Each set of gear included two wagons, each carrying a Beardslee telegraph instrument. Reels, grounding rods, and splicing tools were included, along with enough insulated wire for the wagons to be stationed five miles apart. Mass production brought so quick a drop in cost that a complete field telegraph system could be purchased for $2,500 in 1862 in the North.

Small arms were considered essential for dress and parade if not for use in battle. A Federal cavalry saber, complete with sheath, usually cost about $7.

Dress swords, much in demand for ceremonial purposes, ran from a low of about $125 to a high of more than $2,500. Most elegant weapons of this sort were presented to high-ranking officers by citizens of their states or by men in their command.

Far more effective as weapons than mass-produced sabers or hand-worked swords, pistols turned out by Starr and by Colt brought about $25 in 1861. So many of them were produced that the price of Colt's army .44-caliber dropped to $13.75. By war's end, plenty of five- and six-chamber weapons were on the market at $12 or a trifle less.

Produced in quantity but never used in battle, pikes were probably the war's most useless weapons. In 1862 Gov. Joseph E. Brown of Georgia made it known that he wanted tens of thousands of pikes. At least one hundred manufacturing firms rushed to turn out the six- or seven-foot poles with twelve-inch pointed blades at about $5 apiece.

In 1862 a New Orleans firm contracted to furnish the Confederate secretary of war with seventy-five tons of gunpowder at 84¢ per pound in gold or silver. Although the conflict was little more than six months old, the company balked at furnishing powder for less than $1.14 per pound in Confederate currency. By the end of 1862 a one-hundred-pound keg of gunpowder smuggled into a seceded state from Europe brought about $300.

Before the war, a shipment of ten thousand muskets cost $2 each. If purchased in smaller quantities, the price was $2.50. Two years later, however, U.S. government officials proudly reported that the Springfield Armory could turn out muskets for about $9. Similar weapons produced by private firms in the North retailed in the $20 range.

Overseas, musket makers charged whatever the traffic would bear. Demand for smoothbores dropped sharply when rifled barrels came into general use, so a Prussian manufacturer dumped eighteen thousand weapons on the world market at $4 each.

At war's end, the Ordnance Department of the U.S. Army announced that any soldier who wanted to keep his weapon could do so for a price. By that time a musket of any kind, with or without accouterments, was valued at $6.

I. P. Lindsay, an employee of the Springfield Armory, developed and patented a vastly improved musket late in 1860. Limited numbers of the .58-caliber muzzleloaders that fired two shots were made and sold. One lot consisting of one thousand pieces went to the U.S. War Department in August 1864 at $25 apiece.

Prices declined steadily after 1860. For 1861–65 the average cost of a musket was only $14.93. With ramrod, bayonet, and other equipment added, many purchasers paid as much as $20 for "a rifled musket of Springfield pattern" that weighed almost ten pounds. Samuel Colt's first large order for this weapon came late in July 1861, calling for the delivery of twenty-five thousand Springfield rifles to the U.S. War Department.

Desperate for the necessary war matériel to sign contracts without haggling, War Department officials paid importer C. K. Garrison $27 each for ten thousand rifled muskets of the Liege variety.

Breechloading weapons with rifled barrels, or rifle-muskets, were abundant by 1862. Early in September, Herman Boker and Company of New York City offered a lot of one hundred thousand guns for $18 each.

Eli Whitney's fame rests upon the invention of the cotton gin, but he also pioneered the use of interchangeable parts. [AUTHOR'S COLLECTION]

During the war the Springfield Armory turned out immense numbers of .577-caliber rifle-muskets. With the output of private industries added, at least 1.5 million were produced.

Eli Whitney is credited with developing the use of interchangeable parts, causing the price of firearms to drop sharply. He believed that $20 was a reasonable price for a musket, and he agreed to produce twenty-five thousand for the military. Before the last rifled musket was ready for use, corporate records show that this contract resulted in a substantial loss for Whitney.

Breechloading rifles were viewed suspiciously by the U.S. War Department when they became available in quantity because it was thought that they'd use too much ammunition. Despite this factor, many individual soldiers and numerous companies or regiments on both sides purchased such rifles with their own money. Thousands were sold at $28 to $30 each.

Inventor Samuel Colt developed a "revolving" rifle in 1857.
[UNIVERSITY OF OKLAHOMA LIBRARY]

When the Spencer repeating rifle was introduced, it initially brought $35. Prices dropped to $29 and then to $20. Battlefield use of this weapon and its competitors demonstrated that the muzzle-loading musket was obsolete. As a result, the U.S. War Department paid $28 each for sixteen thousand breechloading carbines of the Gibbs variety.

Samuel Colt's revolving rifle brought $50 in 1857. Although the Colt rifle usually cost $45, many who used this splendid weapon considered it worth twice as much as the best Gibbs ever made.

A Colt was cheap by comparison with the telescope-equipped rifle handmade in Boston by W. G. Langdon. A veteran maker of watches and clocks, Langdon's heavy rifle was designed especially for snipers. He finished only a few pieces, but sold twenty of them to the U.S. War Department for $150 each.

Immediately after the loss at Bull Run, U.S. Secretary of War Simon Cameron contacted an arms buyer in New York. It was imperative, he wrote, to take a fast ship to Europe and purchase one hundred thousand rifled muskets. In addition, Cameron wanted ten thousand carbines and the same number of revolvers. For the massive purchasing program he established a $2 million line of credit.

Confederate agents had already bought the best that England and Europe had to offer. As a result, the hurried trip yielded only fifteen thousand English-made Enfield rifles whose average cost was $18.45. An additional four thousand decidedly inferior French-made rifles were picked up at nearly $17 apiece.

For New York troops, the same purchasing agent secured twenty-five thousand Enfield rifled muskets, for which he paid only $16.70. Although large quantities of Austrian-made pieces were on the market at $10, comparatively few of these inferior weapons reached Federal forces.

U.S. manufacturers never forgot that superior rifles were in great demand. By 1864 a .44 Henry rifle with a fifteen-cartridge magazine was selling for $35.

Only a handful of wealthy soldiers could afford to buy the Whitworth target rifle. Imported by Tiffany's of New York, this handmade weapon, equipped with a telescopic sight, was considered a bargain at $1,250.

After the last bullet was fired, any Union combat veteran could buy a fine Spencer carbine from the War Department for $10. Other carbines were tagged at $8.

"Galvanized Yankees," or Confederates who took the oath of loyalty and changed sides, were mostly used for guard duty on the frontier. As a special reward for their services, in 1866 this small group of veterans was offered an opportunity to buy Springfield rifles for $6 each.

A few analysts have published estimates of the number of cartridges expended during the conflict. In the case of major Northern manufacturers, some accurate records are available. A report issued by the Winchester Company indicated that it produced 58,238,924 cartridges of the Spencer variety alone.

Bullets were produced in scores of types and varieties. When fighting forces withdrew from Gettysburg, early relic hunter J. M. Bush picked up 125 different kinds of bullets on the battlefield.

A horse depot near Washington. [HARPER'S WEEKLY]

Ebenezer Starr, a carbine maker in Yonkers, New York, in 1861 put cartridges on the market at $24.95 per thousand. Six months later "musket shells" were bringing $150 per thousand in New Orleans.

When cartridges with flanged copper cases for use in carbines became available in quantity, three firms controlled the market. With demand from the War Department estimated to be 42,350,000 in 1864, manufacturers offered them in lots of ten thousand at a price of $280.

Horses constituted a source of major expense for the U.S. government and for some individual owners. During the summer of 1861 the War Department customarily paid an average of $120 per animal. Within two years, a healthy animal could not be purchased for less than $150. During 1864, the price in the North was stabilized at $170.

Robert E. Lee saw an attractive colt during the spring of 1862. Having purchased the animal for $200, he named him Traveller.

Since prices were not stabilized in the South, they soared to astronomical heights. In 1863 owners of stables in Richmond had no difficulty filling their stalls with animals whose owners paid $300 a month for their keep. Early in 1865 a Confederate cavalryman seldom found anyone willing to curry his mount for less than $400 in currency.

The cost of food for horses soared as the war dragged on. In the spring of 1861, plenty of corn was available in El Paso at $3.50 per bushel. By 1865 those few farmers who had managed to hoard a supply of grain doled it out for 25¢ to 50¢ an ear.

Civilians everywhere were caught in the price squeeze, which became far more acute in the South than in the North. Quinine was sold for $5 an ounce in New York in 1862, while the same quantity was eagerly grabbed up in South Carolina for $60. During the two years of conflict that followed, a Confederate lucky enough to find quinine for sale had to pay $400 to $600 an ounce. Meanwhile the typical country doctor in the South raised his fee for a house call from $1 to $30.

When flannel jumped to $20 a yard in Petersburg, many potential purchasers protested. Before the conflict ended, it was not unusual for a handkerchief to bring $20. Bonnets and hats became virtually unobtainable in the Confederacy; when a nice piece of headgear was brought in by a blockade-runner in 1864 it was likely to be priced at $500 or more.

Flour, a necessity for soldiers as well as civilians, provides an inflation index of sorts. Much of it was sold in barrels that held about 125 pounds. As late as the spring of 1862, a barrel of flour could be purchased in New York for $6; the same quantity cost about $25 on the New Orleans market. Six months earlier the price in New Orleans had been $18, but flour produced in Spain was available there at $10. By fall, the residents of Vicksburg found little flour on the market at $20 a barrel.

Richmond's Libby Prison was reserved for captured Federal officers and was full for all four years of the war. [THE SOLDIER IN OUR CIVIL WAR]

In Richmond, where price controls were attempted, a barrel of flour was worth $16 in October 1862. That was $4 less than the going rate at Fort Walla Walla in the Washington Territory.

By January 1863, newspapers in the Confederate capital were advertising flour at $25 per barrel. The inmates of Libby Prison, unable to purchase flour at market prices, were forced to pay $100 to $110. Far to the south, in occupied New Orleans, the price was $60 and rising.

In November 1863 the *Richmond Examiner* bewailed that flour had reached $125 per barrel and it was hoped that this was a peak from which the price would soon recede. The editors were wrong; in the Confederate capital flour doubled in price during the next four months.

During the winter of 1864, anywhere in the Confederacy, a person was lucky to find flour at only $275 per barrel. In Vicksburg, the price had passed $400, a price also common at many inland hamlets. Libby Prison inmates were told that the precious commodity was available in limited quantities at $900 per barrel in hard currency.

By 1865 Confederate officials were paying $1,000 per barrel. One of the worst riots to hit a Confederate city occurred in Richmond when housewives staged a bread riot to protest the high prices. They were dispersed only after Jefferson Davis threatened to call out the troops.

When turpentine glutted the New Orleans market early in 1862, it brought only $3 a barrel, while New York residents were glad to get it at $38.

Bacon was plentiful in Richmond during the spring of 1860, and sellers considered themselves fortunate to get 22¢ per pound. At Fort Walla Walla, the same bacon would have brought 30¢.

Inmates of Libby Prison in Richmond paid 75¢ for bacon during the fall of 1862 and $3.50 just one year later. Shortly before war's end, it jumped to the range of $6.50 to $7 per pound in the Confederate capital.

Salt purchased at Nassau for 60¢ a pound in January 1863 was worth $80 to $100 when it reached a Confederate port aboard a blockade-runner.

Fuel was almost as expensive as salt and quinine. Except in mining regions, where it was plentiful, coal cost about $4 a ton in 1860, rising to $12 and then to $20—when it could be found.

Wood that was worth 50¢ a cord before the war was almost unobtainable in 1865, when it brought $100 in Charleston. Persons living far from a source of wood were forced to buy it by the stick at $5, since sellers were unwilling to part with an entire cord at one time. Kerosene, relatively new on the market, was much more stable in price than were other sources of heat. It increased in price only 13¢ a gallon during four years of war—from 28¢ to 41¢.

During 1861, 99,863 bales of cotton were sold on the Savannah market. For this staple the lowest price of the year was 4¢ a pound and the highest was 14½¢. In June 1862, the price jumped to 50¢ in England.

Long staple or sea-island cotton was much less abundant than the upland or short staple variety. In 1863 only 7,114 bales of premium quality cotton were sold at Savannah, but the price varied from 8¢ a pound to 32¢ during the year.

Very little tobacco, prized by fighting men in both gray and blue, was produced in Union territory. Confederate fighting men who agreed to accept their pay in tobacco instead of currency usually got it at about $1 per pound.

So much of it was available in the South that an inmate of Libby Prison could get it at this price until 1862, when "navy plug" jumped to $2.50. Once rampant inflation caught up with Southerners who had nothing but depreciated Confederate currency, tobacco was considered to be cheap at $15 a pound.

One of the least expensive of Civil War items was also the most widely purchased. Tens of millions of "rations," or allocations of food for a soldier or sailor for one day, were bought, assembled, and distributed. In 1861 a Confederate ration cost 35¢, but by 1865 the cost had soared to $2.50. Initially, a great many Federal rations were secured at 14¢, but continuous increases in the volume of purchases added to relatively little inflation in the North meant that increases in the cost of this all-important commodity were reported only in fractions of a cent.

16

Ransoms, Rewards, and Prizes

No one knows what commander conceived the idea of exacting a ransom for a captured town rather than burn it. Nevertheless, this concept proved to be profitable.

A Federal officer may have been the first to try this. From Hudson, Missouri, on August 19, 1861, a directive was sent "to Mayor and Authorities, City of Palmyra, State of Missouri." These officials were ordered "to deliver up to the military authorities of this brigade, within six days, the marauders who fired upon the train bound west on the Hannibal and Saint Joseph Railroad on the evening of the 16th instant, and broke into the telegraph office."

Since compliance was unlikely, the Union demands ended with an offer of ransom that read: "If the guilty persons are not delivered up as required, and within the time herein specified, the whole brigade will be moved into your county, and contributions levied to the amount of $10,000 on Marion County and $5,000 on the city of Palmyra." The order was signed by Brig. Gen. Stephen A. Hurlbut, "under direction of John Pope, brigadier-general, commanding North Missouri."

Confederate Brig. Gen. John McCausland added a refinement in July 1864. Having demanded a huge collective ransom from the citizens of Chambersburg, Pennsylvania, he then required individual residents and merchants to pay amounts ranging from about $150 to $750. McCausland failed to stress one clause of the agreement, if he mentioned it at all. Regardless of the ransom paid by an individual, if the town itself failed to come up with the entire sum demanded, the whole place would be torched.

Eager to retaliate for the Federals' burning of three Virginia homes, McCausland ordered the evacuation of the village and burned it to the ground. Years later, the state of Pennsylvania paid $1,628,431 to Chambersburg residents as compensation for their losses.

Confederate Brig. Gen. John Hunt Morgan had earlier employed a similar but simpler technique. During his July 1863 raid into Ohio, in Summansville and in Pomeroy he demanded that business owners pay ransoms to save their establishments. Unlike McCausland, Morgan spared the places whose owners paid; he didn't have time to destroy them.

Just before Morgan started toward Cincinnati, Confederate Lt. Gen. Jubal Early and his men took possession of the village of York, Pennsylvania. He would let the place stand, he told the residents, in exchange for payment of ransom. An accommodating Virginian, Early said he'd accept commodities in lieu of some of the cash he badly needed.

Late in the evening of June 28, 1863, the citizens delivered $28,600 in cash and many wagonloads of food, clothing, and shoes. As a result, the town not far from the state capital was returned to its residents intact.

Shortly afterward, Early's men reached Gettysburg and again demanded ransom, this time in the amount of $10,000. They believed the villagers were telling the truth when they said they had little or no money on hand. Thus the Confederates agreed to spare it in return for a ransom consisting of seven thousand pounds of pork, twelve hundred pounds of sausage, one thousand pounds of coffee, six hundred pounds of salt, one thousand pairs of shoes, five hundred hats, sixty barrels of flour, and ten bushels of onions.

While the residents of Gettysburg were trying to assemble the ransom, scouts reported that Federal troops were approaching. This time, the Confederate commander left so hurriedly that he took little or nothing with him. He returned later in a futile attempt to acquire shoes, and this second foraging party precipitated the battle of July 1–3, 1863.

On July 6, 1864, Early's lieutenant McCausland took possession of Hagerstown, Maryland. For a mere $200,000, he said, he would not reduce it to ashes in retribution for Federal depredations in the Shenandoah Valley. There was no way that the folk of Hagerstown could assemble that much money. They did their best, though, and put together $20,000. The Confederate grudgingly accepted it and rode away.

The following day, July 7, Early's troops moved into the tiny hamlet of Middletown, Maryland, and he offered to spare the town in return for a ransom of $5,000. The residents simply didn't have that kind of money, they explained. A hasty door-to-door canvas yielded $1,500. When that ransom was delivered, Middletown escaped the flames.

Headed toward Washington, believed to be lightly defended for a brief period, Early made a short detour. Crossing the Potomac at Sheperdstown, he reached Frederick, Maryland, on July 9, 1864.

For a ransom of $200,000, he would bypass the town. Again the town population decided it was better to borrow than to burn, but Early lost a full day waiting for them to assemble the ransom. As soon as the money was delivered, he charged off to Washington. Some claim that the day's delay allowed the Washington defenses to be warned and better prepared for Early's attack.

Descendants of the townspeople who managed to satisfy Early worked hard for decades to pay off the debt they incurred to meet the ransom. It was a triumphant day when the last of Frederick's indebtedness was paid off eighty-seven years after the town had boosted Confederate coffers by $200,000.

At least one Federal officer seems to have used the ransom ploy to line his own pockets. As post commander at Natchez, Mississippi, Brig. Gen. James M. Tuttle sent his troops to arrest as many prominent citizens as they could find.

Once a man was in captivity, Tuttle contacted his relatives. He claimed to be holding a person suspected of treasonable activities, and demanded a ransom in order to release the suspect. Short of that, the person would be tried and might possibly face the death penalty.

It took the citizens of Frederick, Maryland, almost a century to repay the loan required to satisfy the ransom demanded by Jubal Early's troops. [MARYLAND STATE ARCHIVES]

Numerous reports, telegrams, and letters from and to Tuttle survive. Not one of them, however, includes even a hint as to the total ransom collected at Natchez or what was done with it.

Following long-standing custom, the captain of a captured ship was often permitted to pay a ransom to save it. Otherwise, the vessel was likely to be burned or taken into port and sold at auction.

On October 9, 1862, the Philadelphia-based *Tonawanda* fell prey to the CSS *Alabama*. Capt. Theodore Julius entered into a formal written contract that stated in part: "I am held and firmly bound, and I do hereby bind Thomas P. Cope and Francis R. Cope, owners of the ship [*Tonawanda*] and cargo, their and my heirs, executors, and assigns, well and truly to pay unto the President of the Confederate States of America for the time being, at the conclusion of the present war between the said Confederate States and the United States, the sum of $80,000, current money of the said Confederate States, and the said ship *Tonawanda*, her tackle and apparel, are hereby mortgaged for the payment of this bond."

The Confederate raider Alabama. [LIBRARY OF CONGRESS]

Also in October 1862, Capt. John Saunders ransomed the brigantine *Baron de Castine*. Based in Castine, Maine, the vessel was released when papers were signed by her captain. On December 5 the schooner *Union*, out of Baltimore, was ransomed for $1,500. Earlier, the bark *Investigator* was turned loose in return for a ransom bond of $11,250.

When Confederates captured the mail steamer *Ariel*, it was correctly judged to be worth far more than the big *Tonawanda*. The value of the vessel stemmed in part from the identity of its owner, Cornelius Vanderbilt of New York City. It was ransomed on December 9, 1862, by Capt. A. G. Jones on a promise of payment to the Confederacy of $261,000. Of this sum, $123,000 was considered to be the value of her cargo.

Rewards never reached the level of ransoms pledged for the release of great ships and their cargoes. Owners of runaway slaves frequently advertised for them and promised payment for their capture and return, but such reward offers seldom exceeded $500.

Former slave Harriet Tubman was in a category all by herself. After she had conducted numerous fugitives to Canada via the Underground Railroad, many in the South were eager to see her captured. A person would have collected rewards amounting to $40,000 had he managed to snare her.

Because of the scarcity of food and the resulting need for austerity, citizens of the Confederacy were forbidden to engage in some activities that had been legal earlier. To foster enforcement, small rewards were offered to informers.

Among the Confederate states, ten enacted legislation limiting or outlawing the use of corn, grain, or fruit for purposes of distillation. In South Carolina, a person who reported a neighbor's operation of an illicit still was paid $250.

To encourage production of food crops, several states put quotas upon land that could be used to grow cotton or tobacco. These restrictions were customarily tied to the number of field slaves, or "hands," held by an owner.

Arkansas, the first state to enact legislation of this sort, forbade anyone to plant more than two acres of cotton for every field hand age fourteen or older. Florida limited growth of the fiber-producing plant to one acre per hand between the ages of fifteen and sixty. South Carolina and Georgia each set the limit of cotton fields at three acres for each field hand between the ages of fifteen and fifty-five.

Fines imposed for violation of these edicts ranged from $500 to $5,000, and any person who provided information leading to collection of a fine was usually rewarded with half of it.

Rewards offered for the apprehension of fugitives ranged from huge amounts to small sums. Having stepped into the office made vacant by Lincoln's assassination, President Andrew Johnson was eager to capture Jefferson Davis. As a result, he offered a reward of $100,000, a sum eventually divided among men under the command of Union Brig. Gen. James H. Wilson.

As governor of Tennessee, William "Parson" Brownlow charged that former governor Isham G. Harris, a Confederate, was "a fugitive from justice who departed with all the state's belongings." Brownlow offered a reward of $100,000 for his capture. There is no record that it was ever paid.

In comparison with Davis and Harris, the reward offered for presidential assassin John Wilkes Booth seemed of small consequence.

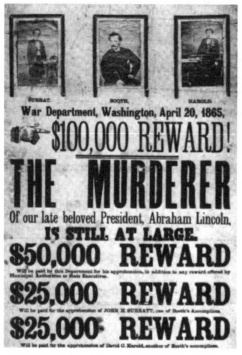

Offers of rewards were posted throughout the District of Columbia and the adjoining states. [LIBRARY OF CONGRESS]

For his capture, U.S. Secretary of War Edwin M. Stanton offered only $50,000.

Stanton also offered to reward the captor of conspirators John H. Surrat and David E. Herold in the sum of $25,000. A separate offer by Col. L. C. Baker of the War Department guaranteed a reward of $30,000 for Booth's capture. Baker's promise, which seems to have been issued without authorization, was based upon belief that Lincoln's killer had unsuccessfully tried to kill U.S. Secretary of State William H. Seward.

Booth was discovered at a Virginia farm and shot during his apprehension. Three officers pulled him from a burning barn and placed him on the porch of the farmhouse where he died. Each of the three officers claimed credit for the capture. For their role in Booth's capture, Capt. Everton J. Conger received $15,000, Lt. Edward P. Doherty received $5,250, and Lt. Luther Baker received $3,750. Sgt. Boston Corbett fired the shot that eventually killed Booth and received a reward of $1,653.85.

Although it was by no means the largest reward posted as an incentive to find or to reveal the whereabouts of a wanted man, the Booth reward is in a special class. All of it was eventually paid, while most other rewards either brought no results or were canceled because of technicalities.

In an aside to the story, a Maj. A. D. Robinson seems to have taken a personal interest in the manhunt for John Wilkes Booth. After the assassin's death was officially reported, he sent Boston Corbett a remittance of $100 that he labeled "a bounty for success in the search for Abraham Lincoln's killer."

During the years in which few persons were neutral and open hostility flourished, anyone and everyone seems to have been permitted to offer a reward for the death or capture of an enemy. In Atlanta, resident George Martin fled after having been charged with uttering "treasonable sentiments against the Southern Confederacy."

In 1861 a group of irate fellow citizens, headed by S. M. Manning, inserted an offer in the town's *Southern Confederacy* newspaper. In it they promised a reward of $250 "for the arrest of Geo. Martin, dead or alive."

Earlier, abolitionist William Lloyd Garrison had evoked the anger of Georgia lawmakers. Years before the outbreak of hostilities, the state legislature enacted a measure perhaps not expected to be taken seriously. Under its terms, any person who brought Garrison to the state was eligible to claim a reward of $1,000.

During fighting near Fort Pickens, Florida, the colorfully garbed members of William Wilson's Zouaves did not always conduct themselves as chivalrous gentlemen. Enraged Confederates blamed what they termed "atrocities" upon Wilson, who headed the unit officially listed as the Sixth New York Infantry.

In October 1861 Wilson's foes posted notices saying that "$5,000 is the reward for him, dead or alive." In a letter he dispatched to New York, Wilson reported, "They are exhibiting my hair and my head in Pensacola—the reward is already claimed."

Operating in western Virginia during the spring of 1862, Union Brig. Gen. Robert H. Milroy encouraged or permitted his men to ruthlessly pillage the area. Furious Confederates in the Tidewater

Pioneer abolitionist and journalist William Lloyd Garrison. [HARPER'S MONTHLY]

region heard of his exploits and offered a reward of $7,500 for his capture.

Confederate Lt. Charles W. Read commanded the commerce raider *Florida* during the spring of 1863. Partly as a result of daring, partly because of exceptionally good luck, Read managed to capture several small merchant ships, fishing schooners, and passenger boats.

Since most of the ships that Read burned were taken in New England waters, Boston merchants banded together and offered a reward of $10,000 for the capture of the Confederate seaman.

An identical sum is reputed to have been offered by Jefferson Davis for the apprehension of Samuel Upson. The man had committed what the Confederate head of state considered to be an especially heinous crime. In Philadelphia, Upson counterfeited Confederate currency that was circulating in Richmond as genuine.

Thomas Garrett of Delaware pretended to be amused when he learned in the prewar years that a price had been put upon his head. Active in work of the Underground Railroad, he was credited with having gained freedom for more than two thousand slaves. Since most of those he aided came from Maryland, the state offered a reward of $10,000 for his capture.

Confederate statesman Clement C. Clay spent more than a year in Canada devising a plan for a negotiated peace. When that effort failed, he returned home and was widely believed to have been implicated in the assassination of Lincoln.

Because he voluntarily gave himself up, no one received the $10,000 reward that had been offered for Clay's capture. After having been held in prison for more than a year without trial, he was released.

Wealthy Richard Yeadon of Charleston was enraged when he learned of Union Maj. Gen. Benjamin F. Butler's actions in occupied New Orleans. Hoping to put an end to those goings-on, Yeadon advertised an offer of a $10,000 reward. It would be paid in Confederate currency, promised the Charlestonian, "for the capture and delivery of the said Benjamin F. Butler, dead or alive, to any proper Confederate authority."

Lt. O. R. McNary of the 103d Pennsylvania Infantry was stationed at Plymouth, North Carolina, during the spring of 1864. As acting superintendent of Negro affairs, he was busily engaged in recruiting former slaves for Federal military forces. According to McNary's postwar account, this activity so offended the Secessionists that an unidentified Confederate provost marshal offered a reward of $10,000 for him, dead or alive.

President Andrew Johnson seems to have discounted reports that the Booth conspiracy originated in or near Washington. Believing that plans for Lincoln's murder had originated in Canada, he offered rewards for a number of prominent Confederates who had operated there.

Johnson's most generous promise was $25,000 to the person or persons who captured Jacob Thompson "within the limits of the United States, so that he can be brought to trial."

At Tammany Hall, Wilson's Zouaves took an oath of fidelity to the flag on April 24, 1861. [HARPER'S HISTORY OF THE CIVIL WAR]

At Charleston in 1863 Confederate Brig. Gen. Thomas Jordan tried to do something about the menacing Federal warships of the Union blockade. Reportedly funded by the international firm of John Fraser and Company, Jordan announced that any person who could show he had been responsible for the sinking of an armored warship would receive a reward of $50,000. Two famous vessels were regarded as especially important. Hence Jordan increased the reward to $100,000 for the destruction of the USS *New Ironsides* or the USS *Wabash*.

Jordan's offers, generous as they were, only echoed others posted in October 1862 by the U.S. Navy Department. With at least a dozen warships searching for the Confederate raider *Alabama,* anyone who could show that he had destroyed the vessel could claim a reward of $300,000. Should a naval officer demonstrate that he was responsible for the capture of the Confederate vessel, a reward of $500,000 was promised.

Two quite different Civil War payments had the same name: bounty. The U.S. government, most states, and many cities and towns offered cash incentives to anyone who volunteered for military service. These bounties became so generous that a new business of bounty brokering evolved. Some brokers became wealthy from a portion of the bounties paid to men they persuaded to enlist—sometimes repeatedly and under assumed names.

Cash payments, usually small, were also offered for the apprehension of persons belonging to specified groups or classes. For example, military officials struggled with the problem of desertion long before the war broke out and offered bounties for the return of anyone who was absent without leave.

On September 7, 1861, the reward for the return of a deserter was reduced from $30 to $5 on grounds that the amount was adequate "to cover all the expenses of apprehension and delivery." Unfortunately, the cut-rate bounty "proved prohibitory to action, and the economy practiced was found in the end to have been expensive." Nearly two years later, with the problem mounting instead of decreasing, the bounty was doubled without producing significant results. During the fall of 1863 a bounty hunter once again received $30 for each deserter.

Before large-scale battles became frequent, the *Mobile Advertiser* published a notice of an offer by the Confederate government. Under its terms, "a premium or bounty of $25 was offered for every prisoner captured and delivered to the authorities by privateers."

A Federal prison on Johnson's Island, Ohio, gained notoriety long before the Confederate prison at Andersonville made headlines. Johnson's Island was three miles from land, and the prison was guarded by a fifteen-foot stockade plus an eight-foot ditch. Nevertheless, so many Confederates escaped that authorities fixed a bounty of $50 on escaped prisoners. Any citizen who captured an escaped prisoner was promised immediate payment.

Cullen M. Baker achieved a record, of sorts, by deserting from both the Confederate and the Union armies. He then recruited a band of followers and set out to pillage villages in Arkansas and Texas.

Cullen was so successful that Gov. Clayton Powell of Arkansas offered a bounty of $1,000 for the capture of "Confederate irregulars," or guerrillas.

At least as early as the fifteenth century, a captured ship was called a prize, this usage stemming from Latin and meaning "to seize." Civil War seamen took the label for granted and used it without explanations for the benefit of landlubbers.

In many instances a victorious captain was too busy to evaluate his capture carefully or lacked the knowledge to do so. Hence many prizes were sent to New Orleans or to Charleston by Confederates and to New York or Philadelphia by Federals, without having price tags placed upon them.

Two vessels captured by the CSS *Sumter* fell into this category. Seized off Puerto Cabello, Venezuela, the *Abby Bradford* went to New Orleans without an appraisal. Sent to "some port on the south side of the island of Cuba" by Raphael Semmes of the same raider, the *Joseph Maxwell* took no estimate of value with her. Until sold at auction, the worth of ships such as these was seldom recorded.

When possible, both Union and Confederate commanders preferred to establish the value of a prize before sending her into port. A system for dividing the money fetched by a capture had been in use for generations. Under its terms, the proceeds from a maritime prize were divided equally between pension funds for seamen and those who effected the capture. Men even remotely involved in a successful assault upon a ship received for their prowess the following allocations:

> Commanding officer of the fleet, 5 percent
>
> Commander of the victorious vessel, 5 percent
>
> Officers above the rank of master, 10 percent
>
> All other officers, 17½ percent
>
> Petty officers, 12½ percent
>
> Seamen, 35 percent

U.S. Secretary of the Navy Gideon Welles was instrumental in abolishing this schedule in 1862. After July 17, officers and seamen who participated in the capture of a prize were rewarded according to the rates at which they were paid.

Frank B. Butts, a paymaster's clerk in the U.S. Navy, was delighted when the blockade steamer *Flag* made a capture. His share of the prize money amounted to $49.97.

Aboard the USS *Nahant,* a powder monkey pocketed $176.16 as his share of the prize money paid by the U.S. government for the CSS *Atlanta.*

Surgeon William F. Hutchinson fared somewhat better. Aboard the U.S. steam sloop-of-war *Lackawanna,* he and his shipmates spotted what they believed to be a Confederate cotton carrier. When the steamer *Isabel* was captured, en route from Galveston to Havana, her hold was packed with 750 bales of cotton. Although the vessel itself was of little value, when the value of its cargo was added to the prize money, Hutchinson's share came to $750.

Youthful William Tillman, cook of the schooner *S. J. Waring,* fared a great deal better. Within weeks of the surrender of Fort Sumter, the Confederate vessel was captured by the privateer *Jeff Davis.* Six men from the *Davis* were put aboard the *Waring* as a prize crew. While most of them were asleep, Tillman went into action. After having killed three men, he persuaded the survivors to surrender.

Once the schooner was in the hands of the cook, soon to be labeled a contraband because of his racial background, he took her into port as a prize of his own. Tillman's exploit, unique in maritime annals of the era, brought him $6,000 in prize money.

Union Adm. Samuel P. Lee of Virginia was distantly related to Robert E. Lee. Joining the U.S. Navy in 1827, he became known as a troublemaker during his first decade on the water. At the outbreak of war he was in command of the USS *Vandalia,* then in South African waters.

Lee did not see any action against the Confederacy and the blockade-runners until his ship returned to U.S. waters and joined the blockading fleet. During the next four years his ship compiled a record that no other came close to matching. Collecting shares totaling $109,689, Lee gained the most prize money in the struggle to drive the blockade-runners out of business.

Officers and seamen in both gray and blue received part of the value of each prize taken by their vessels. One such prize, the sloop *Alligator,* was valued at just $50 when she was captured by the Federal gunboat *Tahoma.*

On December 1, 1861, the crew of the USS *Penguin* rejoiced when the vessel reached New York with the captured schooner *Albion* (formerly the *Lucy R. Waring*) in tow. Since the blockade-runner based at Nassau carried a valuable cargo, her captors divided $100,000 in prize money.

Among the most powerful of Confederate ships, the CSS *Atlanta* was one of the new class of ironclads against which wooden warships had no chance for victory. Because the vessel was considered so formidable, the crew of the Federal warship that captured it divided an even $300,000 in prize money.

Union tars who helped to capture the blockade-runner *Lady Stirling* were distressed when they lost at least seventy-five bales of cotton to a fire caused by their guns. They were elated, however, when they learned that the ship and its remaining cargo were worth $489,891.29.

That sum was topped on November 10, 1863, when the steamer *Memphis* was captured with a heavy load of weapons purchased abroad. Because her cargo was so valuable, this blockade-runner yielded $510,914.07 in prize money to the men of the USS *Magnolia.*

From 1861 to 1865, more than eleven hundred prizes, mostly blockade-runners, were captured by the U.S. Navy. Approximately one-fourth of them were lost at sea, but prize money awarded for those that made it into harbor exceeded $24 million.

On the other hand, there is no formal accounting of those ships that had been ransomed, no way to confirm that the bonds signed by captains of the captured vessels were honored after the vessels had been released.

Four vessels taken in the blockade were central to a vital and long-drawn legal contest. Owners of the *Amy Warwick,* the *Crenshaw,* the *Hiawatha,* and the *Brilliante* sued the government over their seizure. War had not been declared, they pointed out, so the taking of the ships as prizes was illegal.

This issue reached the U.S. Supreme Court in February 1863, after having been delayed so that three newly appointed justices could be seated. The legality of the conflict that the president termed an insurrection was threatened by the charges of the attorneys representing the owners of the four prizes. The quartet of separate actions were labeled "the Prize Cases." Hearings concerning this issue resulted in the only significant Supreme Court ruling during the Civil War.

The justices concluded that although never declared by Congress, a de facto state of war began on Friday, April 19, 1861. Five days after Federal forces surrendered at Fort Sumter, the president made public a proclamation designed "to set on foot a blockade of the ports from South Carolina to Texas."

Soon extended northward along the Atlantic Coast, the blockade was initially unenforceable. Yet the date of its proclamation, taken as having launched a war that existed without having been declared, was named as the starting point of the conflict. This verdict was reached by a five-to-four decision. The dissenting justices argued that a state of war did not exist until July 13, 1861, when Congress recognized that war existed without having been declared.

Once April 19 was legally established as the date on which the conflict began, persons whose ships were seized as prizes could not get compensation. Neither could an agent or agency of the U.S. government be sued for losses incurred after that date.

CHAPTER

17

The Golden Touch

The English poet Thomas Hood died sixteen years before the outbreak of war across the Atlantic. In sixteen lines of a lengthy poem, the Englishman praised and berated gold. Two of the lines give a capsule summary of Civil War attitudes toward the most precious metal then known to western civilization: "Bright and yellow, hard and cold, / Heavy to get, and light to hold."

California was not the site of the earliest U.S. gold rush. It took place in regions destined to be included in the Confederacy— North Carolina and Georgia. So much of the yellow metal came from the hills of North Georgia that a branch of the U.S. Mint was established at Dahlonega. Since gold and silver coins made up the only U.S. legal tender prior to the Civil War, the national supply of metal was a critical issue. Production in California peaked between 1851 and 1857, then fell to an average of about two million ounces annually during the war years.

When the first shell exploded over Fort Sumter, gold pieces were abundant. Eagles, named for the design stamped upon them and first issued in 1795, were worth $10. A double eagle, issued by the U.S. Mint beginning in 1850, was twice as valuable. Half-eagles and quarter-eagles abounded, as did gold $3- and $1-coins. Anyone who didn't have a few pieces of gold in his pocket was indeed poor.

The outbreak of war soon led to hoarding, causing more and more gold coins to disappear from circulation. This situation was exacerbated when the U.S. Treasury began to print greenbacks that were not redeemable in gold. This device, designed to multiply the perception of national wealth, led to depreciation of currency everywhere. In the Confederacy, the crisis reached monumental levels just before the surrender at Appomattox. In the Union, matters were not as bad, but they could have been a lot better in 1865 when $236 million in greenbacks were in circulation.

Despite the eventual success in converting money usage from metal to paper, during the Civil War Americans nevertheless valued gold more highly than ever before. Such a state of affairs inevitably triggered many ploys and capers. Although the amount involved varied widely, the yellow metal sparked intrigue wherever it appeared.

Washington was briefly exultant when gold was found in the Montana Territory late in May 1863. This find did not compare with the California strike, but it was sufficient to grease the wheels of the Federal war machine for a few days.

A correspondent of the *Richmond Sentinel,* while bemoaning the Federal godsend, was inspired by it. He challenged all loyal Confederates to turn their gold and silver plate over to the government. This "vast and unproductive fund," he wrote, "might be made to act a valuable subsidiary part in any well-digested scheme to restore the credit of the Treasury."

Despite his fervent appeal, there is no record that a significant amount of household gold was sent to Richmond. All through the seceded states, folk responded more readily when requested to turn in church bells so they could be used in making guns and ammunition.

By March 1863 citizens residing in the Confederate capital were offering $400 in currency for $100 in gold. Thirty days later, a person was lucky to get five double eagles for $500. In Atlanta a full year before Sherman arrived, a single eagle jumped in value to $121.10 in July 1863.

Clark Wright of the Ninth New York Zouaves wrote: "In September, 1861, $1.10 of Confederate money was equal to $1 in United States gold." By January 1865, it took $60 Confederate money to buy $1 in gold.

That did not mean the Confederacy was entirely without gold. When Jefferson Davis and his close associates fled from Richmond, they took with them a few wagons heavy with gold. Capt. Micah H. Clark, acting treasurer of the Confederacy, never said how much gold went south. Like everyone else, he probably did not know.

At Abbeville, South Carolina, the bullion is supposed to have been transferred to the care of Brig. Gen. Basil Duke. Since it was not with Davis when he was captured in Georgia, it was stolen or hidden somewhere in the South. To this day, hopeful hunters continue to pore over clues considered likely to point them to where the Confederate treasure was stashed.

Racing toward what he hoped would be freedom, Jefferson Davis soon outdistanced what was left of the Confederate treasury. A short special train bearing some or all of it reached Danville, Virginia, on April 5, 1865.

Men assigned to guard the treasure wanted to leave it in Danville, but no officer of the James River Squadron was authorized to accept it. As a result, the treasure train pulled out for Charlotte, North Carolina, still carrying an estimated $200,000 in silver and $300,000 in gold.

Although Davis was rumored to be in Charlotte, he could not be found. Again, guardians of the treasure were frustrated because no one was willing to accept it. As a result, the treasure train slowly snaked its way into the Deep South and oblivion.

Although no one knows exactly how much gold left Richmond hurriedly in April 1865, Lt. Warren H. Mead of the Sixth Kentucky Cavalry never forgot the exact amount he received ninety days earlier.

Captured and shipped from one stockade to another, Mead wound up at "Camp Sorghum," adjacent to Columbia, South Carolina. After guards instructed him, he drew a draft upon his father. The terms of the instrument made Lockwood Mead of Genoa, Cayuga County, New York, liable for $50 in gold. In return for the draft, the prisoner of war was handed a blue slip of paper worth $399.99 in Confederate currency.

Mead turned the bulk of his money into extra provisions. With "a piece of poor fresh beef the size of a man's hand ranging in price from $14 to $17.50," during the fifteen days before the prisoners were liberated by Sherman's forces, Mead spent more than two hundred Confederate dollars on meat and sweet potatoes.

Surgeon William F. Hutchinson was serving a hitch on the USS *Lackawanna* at the time Mead found that a draft on his father was as good as gold. His vessel, part of the West Gulf Blockading Squadron, saw many a blockade-runner make it safely into port. A woman once visited the Federal warship under a flag of truce. Complimented upon the appearance of the calico dress she wore, the Texas woman tossed her head before responding, "It sure ought to look great. Last week it cost me my last $200 in gold." When that dress was purchased, food for an officer aboard the *Lackawanna* cost about twenty-five U.S. dollars weekly.

In a little-known caper, a quartet of French adventurers left Washington late in March 1862. Their destination was Richmond, where they planned to kidnap Jefferson Davis. Traveling under assumed names selected from Alexander Dumas's *The Three Musketeers*, they reached Manassas without difficulty.

At the spot made famous in July 1861, "Porthos" managed to shoot himself in the hand with his pistol. That forced him to give up the adventure, but his companions pressed on toward their target.

Deciding that they could not make it without horses, the three remaining Frenchmen bargained with a Virginia farmer. The man had three good horses he was willing to sell, but he declined to take the trio's greenbacks. He did, however, provide them with mounts when they produced $300 in gold. As the farmer pocketed the specie, he pointed out the road to Fredericksburg as a gesture of goodwill. Neither the horses nor the goodwill did the trio much good; they were discovered by a Confederate patrol and returned to Washington.

Early in 1864, notorious guerrilla leader William C. Quantrill conceived a plot similar to that of the Frenchmen. With a handful of followers, he set out for Washington to kidnap or kill Lincoln. On May 10, in Kentucky, his men clashed with Federal troops.

Mortally wounded, the Ohio native who had earlier plundered Lawrence, Kansas, survived for twenty days. Moaning on his deathbed, Quantrill produced a pouch crammed with what remained of his fortune.

When Kate Clarke, Quantrill's lover, visited the prisoner, he handed her everything he had—$500 in gold. Kate did not wait for him to die; she took the first coach to Saint Louis and used the gold to set up a brothel.

Robert Toombs, one of Georgia's wealthiest planters, saw much that he had accumulated evaporate. During his years as a Confederate brigadier and as the Confederacy's secretary of state, his fortune dwindled to about 10 percent of its prewar level. That did not prevent the fiery attorney from continuing to treat gold casually.

Upon his return to civilian life, Robert Toombs refused to take the required oath of allegiance to the Union. [GEORGIA HISTORICAL SOCIETY]

After the last Confederate cabinet meeting was held in Washington, Georgia, members of the Fourth Illinois Cavalry seized the town. Busy paroling prisoners, Capt. Lot Abraham barely looked up when a visitor approached him.

"My name is Toombs," he said as though he expected everyone to be familiar with it. "In passing my house a few days ago, Breckinridge threw down from his horse a meal sack. When I picked it up, it was found to be very heavy. That sack held $1,780 in gold and $3,400 in silver. Looks as though it might belong to your government; here, take it."

Startled, the Federal officer asked no questions. Had he done so, he might have concluded that the precious metal stuffed in the meal sack was part of the lost treasure of the Confederacy.

Spy extraordinary Rose Greenhow O'Neal went to England after being banished from the United States. Probably serving as a Confederate courier, she remained there until entrusted with top-secret papers. En route to Wilmington aboard a blockade-runner, O'Neal feared capture when a Federal vessel approached. With two companions she took to a rowboat.

Heavy seas sent the rowboat to the bottom as it came close to shore. O'Neal might have escaped had she not been wearing a

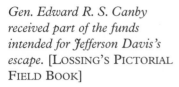

Gen. Edward R. S. Canby received part of the funds intended for Jefferson Davis's escape. [LOSSING'S PICTORIAL FIELD BOOK]

money belt stuffed with at least $2,000 in gold. The precious metal claimed the life of the skilled and colorful espionage agent.

Tradition has it that a Confederate soldier found the body of the dead woman and emptied the fatal money belt. When he discovered her identity, he reputedly turned the gold over to the Confederate authorities.

After the surrender at Appomattox, Confederate Brig. Gen. Edmund Kirby-Smith, head of the Trans-Mississippi Department, had hoped to assist Jefferson Davis in his escape from the collapsing Confederacy. The Confederate president, however, was captured on May 10 in Georgia, and Kirby-Smith surrendered the last Confederate bastion on May 26.

Kirby-Smith had been holding $5,000 in gold for the former president's personal expenses. As his men had not been paid in weeks, the general took out 340 gold eagles to be divided "on salary account." The remaining gold was sent to Brig. Gen. Edward R. S. Canby in New Orleans as "the balance of the secret service fund of the Trans-Mississippi Department." Flat broke, Kirby-Smith borrowed $100 in Confederate currency with which to make his way home.

Attorney Philip Phillips of Washington seems to have been ignorant of the activities of his wife, Eugenia. Having come under the influence of Rose Greenhow O'Neal, she had joined a spy ring early in 1861. Seized late in the summer, Eugenia and her sister were placed under house arrest in the O'Neal home.

Phillips, whose practice was limited to cases bound for the U.S. Supreme Court, spent at least three weeks cajoling prominent officials. Eventually the women were given permission to enter the Confederacy by way of Fortress Monroe.

Lt. Gen. Winfield Scott personally made arrangements for the former prisoners to take a steamboat headed for the South. As a gesture of personal appreciation for a respected attorney whose loyalty to the Union was never questioned, he permitted Phillips to leave the Federal capital with $5,000 in gold.

At Catlett's Station, Virginia, J. E. B. Stuart staged a spectacular raid in August 1862. Leading fifteen hundred cavalrymen in gray, he seized the headquarters of the Army of Virginia.

Much of the loot found near the residence of Union Maj. Gen. John Pope was routine, but chests intended for use by paymasters were not. When he returned to his own lines, Stuart carried with him $20,000 in gold. To subordinates he confessed that he considered this haul to be far more exciting than the $500,000 in greenbacks also captured.

Confederate Brig. Gen. James E. Slaughter was among claimants for the honor of having fought in the last battle of the war. After failing to score a victory at Palmito Ranch, Texas, he withdrew across the Rio Grande. There he soon sold his artillery to Mexican Maj. Gen. Tomas Meija, who paid for his purchase with $20,000 in gold.

Alabama cotton broker Zachariah Deas was known to be well off financially. When the state's Twenty-second Regiment was formed in the fall of 1861, Deas yearned to be its colonel. He found it easy to gain the coveted spot but was surprised to learn that his men were not ready to fight. Some of them had no weapons, and the rest were armed with muskets and squirrel rifles.

The regiment's leader immediately ordered a shipment of splendid Enfields, which he paid for with $28,000 in gold. A grateful government later reimbursed Colonel Deas with $28,000

The ranking general of the army at the beginning of the war, Winfield Scott held that position until George B. McClellan was awarded that position by Lincoln. [LESLIE'S ILLUSTRATED]

in Confederate bonds that became worthless not long after they were printed.

Analysts of the northernmost of Confederate raids have uncovered aspects of the story that were unknown in October 1864. Bank records recently uncovered indicate that the men who robbed Saint Albans, Vermont, were hasty and careless, to say the least. Making their getaway to Canada, they left behind at least $50,000 in gold.

The soldiers who robbed the Vermont banks were also guilty of sloppy planning. Hence most of them were soon captured on Canadian soil and were found to be carrying $88,000 in U.S. currency.

Since the money was part of the capture, it became Canadian property. Public outcry north of the border soon forced the passage of unique legislation. Under its terms, three Saint Albans banks were eventually paid $50,000 in gold by the Canadian government.

Confederate Brig. Gen. Albert Pike was concerned during the harsh winter of 1861–62 that his men had not been paid for months. Trying to remedy the situation, he dispatched his son, Walter, to Richmond. When military officials were presented with demands from a leader they badly needed in the West, they expedited Walter's return to Arkansas with $63,000 in gold.

Federal forces seemed ready to pounce upon Pike's troops when the payroll funds arrived. Desperate to safeguard his money, the Confederate entrusted it to a slave known only as Brutus with instructions to hide it.

Two days after the March 7–8 battle of Pea Ridge, or Elkhorn Tavern, a solitary bedraggled black man guided his horse into the Confederate camp. When the slave handed over the gold-filled bag, he was rewarded with his freedom on the spot.

On May 27, 1862, Confederate Secretary of the Treasury C. G. Memminger drafted a unique memo to Jefferson Davis. He reported that $100,000 in gold that had been designated for the ordnance department had been seized in Mobile, Alabama, by Gen. P. G. T. Beauregard. The officer who had executed the general's order, Lt. Col. Frank H. Hatch, explained that this had been done to prevent the money's falling into enemy hands. Normally, when a Confederate horde was seized by Southern forces, the money was returned to the treasury in Richmond.

As military governor, Union Maj. Gen. Benjamin F. Butler ruled New Orleans with a high hand. Documents of the period strongly support claims that he considered any money he uncovered to be the property of the U.S. government.

At the office of the consul of the Netherlands, some of Butler's aides became suspicious when they noticed a number of kegs. An attempt to move a single keg evoked a one-word signal: Money!

Once in Federal hands, the keg that seemed strangely out of place in the office of a consul yielded $5,000 in gold. So did each of 159 other kegs seized in a violation of international law that enriched the U.S. Treasury by $800,000.

Weapons, quinine, shoes, and other badly needed commodities were the backbone of the blockade-running business. One of them, the *Giraffe*, was renamed the *Robert E. Lee* soon after having been purchased for the unusually large sum in 1862 of $160,000 in gold.

Officers and men aboard the new member of the Confederate fleet bragged that the steamer built in England was the fastest

Christopher G. Memminger was the first Confederate secretary of the treasury. [BATTLES AND LEADERS]

vessel afloat. That boast, seldom challenged, was repeated during twenty-one successful voyages. Before being captured she took to English markets at least seven thousand bales of cotton worth more than $2 million in gold.

With Confederate currency depreciating rapidly, Secretary of the Treasury C. G. Memminger concocted a scheme designed to create financial panic in the North. By buying gold in quantity and exporting it, he believed that he could create a fiscal crisis.

A plea to Southern sympathizers in loyal states was linked with the plot. Urged to convert paper money into gold and horde it, many citizens acted promptly.

At the same time, Confederate agent J. Porterfield went from Montreal to New York and began buying gold for export. He managed to ship about $2 million out of the country before a partner was arrested. This ended the Confederacy's great gold caper.

In May 1864, Joseph Howard, city editor of the *Brooklyn Eagle,* conceived a scheme designed to make himself rich almost overnight. His first step was to buy gold with every dollar he could borrow. Then he fed bogus news stories concerning a Federal call for an additional four hundred thousand men to numerous publications. Two of them, the *New York World* and the *Journal of Commerce* took the bait detailing military failures necessitating the draft. When readers absorbed the dismal news, many began to buy gold as a hedge against inflation. The price of gold jumped 10 percent in a single day. Now famous as the Gold Hoax, the plot masterminded by a newspaper editor did not make him rich. Instead, it sent him to jail for ninety days.

In Washington, the gold scare caused Lincoln to suffer one of the most serious embarrassments of his presidency. He *had* planned to issue just such a call as Howard described, but furor created by the Gold Hoax forced him to delay the proclamation for two months.

Selected
Bibliography

Abdill, George B. *Civil War Railroads*. New York: Bonanza, 1961.
Abraham Lincoln Quarterly. 15 vols. Urbana: University of Illinois Press, 1979–94.
American Annual Cyclopedia and Register of Important Events (Appleton's). New York: Appleton, 1861–65.
American Heritage. New York, 1948–95.
America's Civil War. Leesburg, Va., 1988–95.
Andrews, J. Cutler. *The North Reports the Civil War*. Pittsburgh: University of Pittsburgh Press, 1959.
———. *The South Reports the Civil War*. Princeton, N.J.: Princeton University Press, 1970.
Annals of the Civil War, The. Philadelphia: Philadelphia Weekly Times, 1879.
Army of the Potomac. *Report of the Joint Committee on the Conduct of the War*. Washington, D.C.: Government Printing Office, 1863–66.
Baker, LaFayette C. *History of the U.S. Secret Service in the Late War*. Philadelphia: L. C. Baker, 1867.
Ball, Douglas B. *Financial Failure and Confederate Defeat*. Urbana: University of Illinois Press, 1991.
Barnard, John G. *A Report on the Defenses of Washington*. Washington, D.C.: Government Printing Office, 1871.
Barton, William E. *President Lincoln*. 2 vols. Indianapolis: Bobbs-Merrill, 1933.
Basler, Roy P., ed. *The Collected Works of Abraham Lincoln*. 8 vols. New Brunswick, N.J.: Rutgers University Press, 1963.
Beller, Susan P. *Medical Practices in the Civil War*. Cincinnati: Betterway, 1992.

Benjamin, Marcus. *Washington During War Time*. Washington, D.C.: National Tribune, 1902.

Blue & Gray. Columbus, Ohio. 1984–95.

Boatner, Mark M. *The Civil War Dictionary*. Revised edition. New York: David McKay, 1988.

Caffey, Thomas E. *Battlefields of the South*. New York: J. Bradburn, 1864.

Canby, Courtland, ed. *Lincoln and the Civil War*. New York: Brazillier, 1960.

Carpenter, Frank B. *Six Months at the White House with Abraham Lincoln*. New York: Hurd and Houghton, 1866.

Catton, Bruce. *The Coming Fury*. Garden City, N.Y.: Doubleday, 1961.

———. *Grant Takes Command*. Boston: Houghton Mifflin, 1968.

———. *Mr. Lincoln's Army*. Garden City, N.Y.: Doubleday, 1962.

———. *Never Call Retreat*. Garden City, N.Y.: Doubleday, 1965.

———. *A Stillness at Appomattox*. Garden City, N.Y.: Doubleday, 1953.

———. *The Terrible Swift Sword*. Garden City, 1963.

Century Magazine. New York: Century, 1878–80.

Chase, Salmon P. *Diary and Correspondence of Salmon P. Chase*. 2 vols. Washington, D.C.: Government Printing Office, 1903.

Chesnut, Mary Boykin. *A Diary from Dixie*. Edited by Ben Ames Williams. Boston: Houghton Mifflin, 1905.

Civil War. Berryville, Va., 1982–94.

Civil War Chronicles. New York: American Heritage, 1991–92.

Civil War Times and *Civil War Times Illustrated*. Harrisburg, Pa., 1959–95.

Confederate Veteran. Nashville, 1893–1932. *Cumulative Index*. 3 vols. Wilmington, N.C.: Broadfoot, 1986.

Connelly, Thomas L. *Army of the Heartland*. Baton Rouge: Louisiana State University Press, 1967.

———. *Autumn of Glory*. Baton Rouge: Louisiana State University Press, 1971.

Coulter, E. Merton. *The Confederate States of America, 1861–65*. Baton Rouge: Louisiana State University Press, 1950.

Current, Richard N., ed. *Encyclopedia of the Confederacy*. 4 vols. New York: Simon & Schuster, 1993.

Cushman, Pauline. *The Romance of the Great Rebellion*. New York: Wynkoop & Hallenbeck, 1864.

Dana, Charles A. *Recollections of the Civil War*. New York: Appleton, 1902.

Davis, Jefferson. *The Rise and Fall of the Confederate Government*. Richmond: Garrett and Massie, 1881.

Davis, William C. *The Imperiled Union.* Garden City, N.Y.: Doubleday, 1982–83.

———, ed. *The Image of War.* 6 vols. Garden City, N.Y.: Doubleday, 1981–84.

Devens, Richard M. *The Pictorial Book of Anecdotes and Incidents of the War of the Rebellion.* Hartford: Hartford, 1866.

Donald, David. *Divided We Fought.* New York: Macmillan, 1952.

Dumont, Dwight L., comp. *Southern Editorials on Secession.* New York: Century, 1931.

Dupuy, R. Ernest. *The Compact History of the Civil War.* New York: Hawthorne, 1960.

Duyckinch, Everet A. *National History of the War for the Union.* New York: n.p., 1867.

Dyer, Frederick H. *A Compendium of the War of the Rebellion.* Des Moines: Frederick H. Dyer, 1908.

Early, Jubal A. *The Campaigns of Gen. Robert E. Lee.* Baltimore: J. Murphy, 1872.

Eaton, Clement. *A History of the Southern Confederacy.* New York: Macmillan, 1954.

Eisenchemiel, Otto, and Ralph Newman. *The Civil War.* Indianapolis: Bobbs-Merrill, 1947.

———. *Why the Civil War?* Indianapolis: Bobbs-Merrill, 1958.

Evans, Clement A., ed. *Confederate Military History.* 17 vols. Atlanta: Confederate, 1899. (Two-volume index: Wilmington, N.C.: Broadfoot, 1987).

Famous Adventures and Prison Escapes of the Civil War. New York: Century, 1893.

Farrar, Fernando. *Johnny Reb.* Richmond: Nye, 1869.

Faust, Patricia, ed. *Historical Times Illustrated Encyclopedia of the Civil War.* New York: Harper and Row, 1986.

Fiske, John. *The Mississippi Valley in the Civil War.* Boston: Houghton Mifflin, 1900.

Foote, Shelby. *The Civil War.* 3 vols. New York: Random House, 1958–86.

Freeman, Douglas Southall. *Lee's Lieutenants.* 3 vols. New York: Scribner's, 1972.

———. *R. E. Lee.* 4 vols. New York: Scribner's, 1934–35.

Frost, Griffin. *Camp and Prison Journal.* Quincy, Ill.: Quincy Journal, 1867.

Fuller, John F. *The Generalship of Ulysses S. Grant.* London: Murray, 1929.

Grant, Ulysses S. *Personal Memoirs of U. S. Grant.* 2 vols. New York: C. L. Webster, 1885.

Guest, James W. *Love, Honor, and Civil War.* Columbia, S.C.: Palmetto Press, 1993.

Haguina, Parthenia. *A Blockaded Family.* Boston: Houghton Mifflin, 1888.

Hall, Charles B. *Military Records of General Officers, C.S.A.* New York: Lockwood, 1898.

Hamersley, Lewis R. *Records of Living Officers of the U.S. Navy and Marine Corps.* Philadelphia: Lippincott, 1870.

Hattaway, Herman, and Archer Jones. *How the North Won.* Urbana: University of Illinois Press, 1983.

Ingraham, Prentiss. *The Two Flags.* New York: n.p., 1897.

Jackson, Florence. *The Black Man in America.* New York: Watts, 1972.

Jackson, John S. *Diary of a Confederate Soldier.* Columbia: University of South Carolina, 1990.

Johnson, Robert V., and Clarence C. Buell, eds. *Battles and Leaders of the Civil War.* 4 vols. New York: Century, 1887.

Johnson, Rossiter. *Campfire and Battlefields.* New York: Civil War Press, 1967.

Johnston, Joseph E. *Narrative of Military Operations During the Late War Between the States.* New York: Appleton, 1874.

Jones, Virgil. *The Civil War at Sea.* 3 vols. Wilmington, N.C. Broadfoot, 1990.

Journal of the Confederate Historical Society. Essex, England, 1962–72.

Journal of the Southern Historical Society. 49 vols. Wilmington, N.C.: Broadfoot: 1990–92. 2-volume index.

Katcher, Philip. *The Civil War Source Book.* New York: Facts on File, 1992.

Ketchum, Robert M. *American Heritage Picture History of the Civil War.* Garden City, N.Y.: Doubleday, 1960.

Knox, Thomas W. *Camp Fire and Cotton Field.* New York: n.p., 1865.

Koerner, Gustave. *Memoirs.* Edited by T. J. McCormick. 2 vols. Cedar Rapids: Torch, 1909.

Lanier, Robert S., ed. *The Photographic History of the Civil War.* 10 vols. New York: Review of Reviews, 1912.

Leech, Margaret. *Reveille in Washington.* New York: Harper, 1941.

Long, E. B. *The Civil War Day by Day.* Garden City, N.Y.: Doubleday, 1971.

Longstreet, James. *From Manassas to Appomattox.* Philadelphia: Lippincott, 1903.

Lossing, Benjamin J. *Lossing's Pictorial Field Guide to the Great Civil War.* Boston: Nagle, 1889.

McClellan, George B. *McClellan's Own Story.* New York: Charles L. Webster, 1886.

McHenry, Robert, ed. *Webster's Military Biographies.* New York: Dover, 1978.

McPherson, James M. *Battle Cry of Freedom.* New York: Oxford, 1988.

Meade, George G. *Life and Letters of G. Gordon Meade.* New York: Scribner's, 1913.

Meredith, Roy, and Arthur Meredith. *Mr. Lincoln's Military Railroads.* New York, Noreton, 1975.

Miers, Earl S. *The American Civil War.* New York: Golden, 1961.

Military Order of the Loyal Legion of the United States. 61 vols. Wilmington, N.C.: Broadfoot, 1993–95.

Moore, Frank, ed. *The Rebellion Record.* 12 vols. New York: Putnam & Nostrand, 1861–68.

National Almanac and Annual Record, 1860–65. 6 vols. Philadelphia: n.p., 1860–65.

Neely, Mark E. *The Abraham Lincoln Encyclopedia.* New York: McGraw Hill, 1982.

Nevins, Allan. *Ordeal of the Union.* 2 vols. New York: Scribner's, 1947.

————. *The War for the Union.* 4 vols. New York: Scribner's, 1959.

Nicolay, John G., and John Hay. *Abraham Lincoln.* 10 vols. New York: Century, 1890.

Official Documents of the Post Office Department of the Confederate States of America. 2 vols. Holland, Mich.: n.p., 1979.

Official Records of the Union and Confederate Navies in the War of the Rebellion. 30 vols. Washington, D.C.: Government Printing Office, 1894–1927.

Perry, Milton F. *Infernal Machines.* Baton Rouge: Louisiana State University Press, 1965.

Phisterer, Frederick. *Statistical Record of the Armies of the United States.* New York: Scribner's, 1883.

Quarles, Benjamin. *The Negro in the Civil War.* Boston: Little Brown, 1953.

Quint, Alonzo H. *The Potomac and the Rapidan.* Boston: n.p., 1864.

Roller, David C., and Robert W. Twyman. *Encyclopedia of Southern History.* Baton Rouge: Louisiana State University Press, 1968.

Royster, Charles. *The Destructive War.* New York: Knopf, 1991.

Sifakis, Stewart. *Who Was Who in the Civil War.* New York: Facts on File, 1988.

Stepp, John W., and I. William Hill, eds. *Mirror of War.* Washington, D.C.: Evening Star, 1961.

War of the Rebellion: Official Records of the Union and Confederate Armies. 130 vols. Wilmington, N.C.: Broadfoot, 1991–95. 6-volume supplement.

Warner, Ezra S. *Generals in Blue*. Baton Rouge: Louisiana State University Press, 1964.

————. *Generals in Gray.* Baton Rouge: Louisiana State University Press, 1959.

Index

Boldface page numbers indicate illustrations